The Latinx Files

T0385578

Global Media and Race

Series Editor: Frederick Luis Aldama, The Ohio State University

Global Media and Race is a series focused on scholarly books that examine race and global media culture. Titles focus on constructions of race in media, including digital platforms, webisodes, multilingual media, mobile media, vlogs, and other social media, film, radio, and television. The series considers how race—and intersectional identities generally—is constructed in front of the camera and behind, attending to issues of representation and consumption as well as the making of racialized and anti-racist media phenomena from script to production and policy.

Matthew David Goodwin, *The Latinx Files: Race, Migration, and Space Aliens*

Hyesu Park, ed., *Media Culture in Transnational Asia: Convergences and Divergences*

Melissa Castillo Planas, *A Mexican State of Mind: New York City and the New Borderlands of Culture*

Monica Hanna and Rebecca A. Sheehan, eds., *Border Cinema: Reimagining Identity through Aesthetics*

The Latinx Files

Race, Migration, and Space Aliens

MATTHEW DAVID GOODWIN
FOREWORD BY FREDERICK LUIS ALDAMA

Rutgers University Press

New Brunswick, Camden, and Newark, New Jersey, and London

Library of Congress Cataloging-in-Publication Data

Names: Goodwin, Matthew David, author. | Aldama, Frederick Luis, 1969-
    writer of foreword.
Title: The Latinx files : race, migration, and space aliens / Matthew Goodwin;
    foreword by Frederick Luis Aldama.
Description: New Brunswick, New Jersey : Rutgers University Press, [2021] |
    Series: Global media and race | Includes bibliographical references and index.
Identifiers: LCCN 2020035573 | ISBN 9781978815100 (paperback; alk. paper) |
    ISBN 9781978815117 (cloth; alk. paper) | ISBN 9781978815124 (epub) |
    ISBN 9781978815131 (mobi) | ISBN 9781978815148 (pdf)
Subjects: LCSH: Science fiction, Latin American—History and criticism. |
    Extraterrestrial beings in literature. | Literature and race.
Classification: LCC PQ7082.S34 G66 2021 | DDC 860.9/3526912—dc23
LC record available at https://lccn.loc.gov/2020035573

A British Cataloging-in-Publication record for this book is available from the British Library.

♾ The paper used in this publication meets the requirements of the American National
Standard for Information Sciences—Permanence of Paper for Printed Library Materials,
ANSI Z39.48-1992.

www.rutgersuniversitypress.org

Manufactured in the United States of America

For Nahir, Violet, and Enora

Contents

Foreword: Why the Space of the Latinx Speculative Matters

■■■■■■■■■■■■■■■■■■■■■■

FREDERICK LUIS ALDAMA

I love my sci-fi. As a teen, I gorged on all that our local librarian recommended: from Mary Shelly, Ursula K. Le Guin, Octavia Butler, Issac Asimov, and Frank Herbert to Julio Cortázar and Jorge Luis Borges. While over the years I would return to these authors whenever given the chance, today I find myself more and more drawn to the speculative in comic books, television shows, and films. This does not in any way reflect a hierarchy of quality: word-drawing narrative, say, as better than alphabetic narrative. It's simply a question of time. I usually have a few minutes to spare and some energy left at day's end, giving these minutes over to imaginative indulgences in speculative spaces built by comics, television shows, and films. What hasn't changed from my teens to today is the dominant impulse. I go to sci-fi less for the plots and more for the exciting ways that creators build new worlds. I'm fascinated by how different creators extrapolate, reimagine, and reconstruct the building blocks of my everyday reality. I'm especially fascinated by how these newly built storyworlds reconstruct the planet's Brown folx.

Mainstream sci-fi (all media and modes) has a deleterious track record when it comes to imagining our historically underrepresented communities of color: Latinx, African American, Asian American, and Indigenous people. Dip into any moment in the mainstream's deep planetary time and reconstructions of folx of color (when they do happen) and they nearly always appear as sets of binary opposites: as exoticized and sexualized Others a la Pocahontas or as untrustworthy, villainous Others.

I recall here a few emblematic examples of mainstream reel sci-fi's lazy and damaging reconstructions of Latinxs. Barry Sonnenfeld's *Men in Black* (1997) includes as its precredit launch into the story proper the following scene: on the U.S. side of the Mexico/U.S. border, a racist *migra* stops a *coyote* who is transporting undocumented Latinxs. Agent K (Tommy Lee Jones) and Agent D (Richard Hamilton) save the undocumented Latinxs, telling them to continue on their way. They hold back one of the border crossers, however—the poncho-wearing Latinx (Sergio Calderón) who doesn't understand Agent K's Spanish. This undocumented Latinx is sliced open from head to toe, revealing an amphibious, flippered alien named Mikey, who, as it turns out, recently escaped prison. These first few minutes of the film reveal much about how Latinxs are reconstructed. There's the Anglo beneficent paternalism: Agent K's generous gesture to let the undocumented Latinxs go free. There's the Latinx threat narrative: the Latinx as literal alien who stealthily crosses into the United States to cause trouble.

Then we have those sci-fi reel reconstructions of Latinxs that identify the geographic region of Mexico as monstrous. In David Twohy's *The Arrival* (1996) and Ed Gareth *Monsters* (2010), Mexico becomes the home base for space aliens to take over the United States and the planet. In the former, some aliens disguise themselves as gardeners (yes, gardeners) to infiltrate the United States. In the latter, the Godzilla-sized space aliens are contained in Mexico by a giant wall.

When sci-fi reels don't mark Latinxs as alien and threatening, they spin narratives of Latinxs as easy disposables, usually to intensify the audiences' empathy for and appreciation of the Anglo protagonist. I think here of Anna (Elpidia Carrillo) as the disposable Latina in *Predators* (1997) who functions to focus attention on the deft, hunter skills of Dutch (Arnold Schwarzenegger). I think here also of Anya Thorensen (Gina Rodriguez) as the disposable Latina in Alex Garland's *Annihilation* (2018), who exists only to ultimately intensify audience emotion for Anglo cellular biologist Lena (Natalie Portman).

When mainstream sci-fi reels reconstruct Latinxs as safe (alien or otherwise), their roles are usually woven thickly within those age-old stereotypes of the exotic and noble savage Other. Think Zoe Saldana's roles in the *Guardians of the Galaxy* (2014) and *Avatar* (2009). Her Latinidad is contained and made safe through her hyperexoticization, through makeup (green or purple) and scripts that replay the non-White characters as primitive, naïve, and in need of a White savior.

It's not all doom and gloom, of course. The recent spate of *Star Wars* films has featured some notable exceptions. In *Rogue One* (2016), Diego Luna infuses complexity and depth to the role of Cassian Andor—and Luna's insistence that he play the role with his Mexican-accented English adds to this complexity. And in the recent *Star Wars* trilogy (2015–2019), Guatemalan-born Latinx actor Oscar Isaac as Poe softens the *machista* attitude of the Latinx warrior figure with his infusion of a nuanced and affectionate interracial, male-male (John Boyega as Finn) relationship. Disney+ channel's casting of Pedro Pascal as the eponymous hero of its *The Mandalorian* has cleared new spaces for seeing (actually, hearing, as he's only unmasked near the end of Season 1) complex articulations of Latinx masculinities: that one can be a warrior and a loving single parent to a nonbiologically related child; in this case, the child popularly identified by Latinxs in the social media sphere as Yodito.

In television, we're seeing some excellent, even radical, sci-fi reel reconstructions of Latinxs. I think readily of such sci-fi shows as SyFy's *Caprica* (2010), HBO's *Westworld* (2017–), and CBS's *Star Trek: Discovery* (2017—). *Caprica* gives most screen time to developing the complex Adama family (with Esai Morales as Joseph Adama) as ethnoracially persecuted Taurons; the show is set in the future and on other planets, but in a way that serves as a smart allegory to the race relations in our tellurian present. *Westworld* features as one of its central robot protagonists the leader of the robot revolution: gunslinger Hector Escatón (Rodrigo Santoro), who wakes to his exploitation and oppression to rise up against the human world. And *Star Trek: Discovery* gives remarkable amounts of screen time to developing the smart *and* queer Dr. Hugh Culber (Wilson Cruz).

Of course, the real reel innovations in sci-fi storyworld building are happening with Latinxs behind cameras, pencils, pens, and typewriters. There's the notably sophisticated, politically nuanced *transfrontera* cross-border sci-fi films and installation art of Alex Rivera that includes *Sleep Dealer* (2009) as well as *Memorial over General Atomics* and *Lowdrone*. There are the genre-bending, epic-scaled sci-fi narratives of Robert Rodriguez, including *Planet Terror* (2007), *Machete Kills* (2013), *Red 11* (2019), and *Alita: Battle Angel* (2019). Rivera and Rodriguez build complex sci-fi storyworlds that reconstruct all facets of today's Latinx life and culture—and that imagine new ways that our culture will *be* as it grows across the *Américas*. Both directors invite—in fact, *urge*—audiences to imagine the ways we can actively transform this tomorrow for the better and more humane.

With pencil and ink, Latinx creators of comics have been revolutionizing sci-fi narrative spaces—and with head-spinning abundance. With *Rocketo* (2006), Frank Espinosa reconstructs his own Cuban émigré experience in a future where the world is nearly all water, with a few island territories known only to the Mapper, Rocketo. Also taking place on a radically transformed planet, Los Bros Gonzalez (John and Carlos) and Julian Aguilera's multiethnic superhero team speak truth to ecological disaster in *The Elites* (2014–). The adventures and epic battles that energize Jules Rivera's *Valkyrie Squadron* (2018) importantly grow and empower a radical decolonial politics. With *God and Science: Return of the Ti-Girls* (2012), Jaime Hernandez creates a near all-women storyworld, including Latina Penny Century, Espectra, Weeper, Cheetah Torpeda, and Space Queen. In Jaime's speculative comic book space, there's no room for patriarchal familial systems; when there are infants, they're tucked away in belt buckles so the Latinas can kick some *culo*. In my forthcoming *Labyrinths Borne* (with Juan Argil), I imagine a future after The Event where all but the teenagers have perished; we build a storyworld space that imagines the vital creative, intellectual energy of teens, including the protagonist, Luna, who turn to science, philosophy, and literature as a way to positively transform the planet.

Many Latinx comics creators choose to build storyworlds that reconstruct the past, and with this decolonize history textbooks that erase the significant presence of transformative Latinx subjects in deep planetary time and place. Rafael Navarro and Mike Wellman's *Guns A'Blazin'!* rewrites yesteryear's Anglocentric Manifesto destiny narratives by featuring the Latinx Eduardo as a supped-up-roadster time traveling cowboy. And we go back even deeper into planetary time with Daniel Parada's precolonial set superhero adventure, *Zotz: Serpent and Shield* (2011–).

Of course, comics are not the only generative space for the speculative reconstructions of Latinx experiences and subjectivities. There is also the vital and transformative work happening within children's and young adult fictional spaces. For instance, I wanted to create a story that touched on today's caging of Latinx children along the U.S./Mexico border. I wanted it to be an adventure story, however, that drew on the powerfully speculative oral stories Latinxs have heard growing up in the Southwest and Puerto Rico: the myth of the Chupacabra, the goat sucker. Working with illustrator Chris Escobar, I created *The Adventures of Chupacabra Charlie* (2020), which follows the adventures of a learned, vegetarian, adventure-seeking Chupacabra named Charlie. And we're seeing a tremendous outpouring of vital Latinx storyworld building in the YA fictional realm. I think of Daniel José Older and Zoraida Córdova who are radically infusing a Latinx sensibility into their re-creations of *Star Wars* narratives such as *Last Shot: A Han and Lando Novel* (2018) and *Star Wars: Galaxy's Edge: A Crash of Fate* (2019), for instance. I also think of Malka Older—*Infomocracy* (2016), *Null States* (2017), and *State Tectonics* (2018)—who builds pre-Colombian mythologically informed storyworlds that critique our current epidemics of destructive social and political behavior, and affirm new intersectional identities and transformative spaces.

Goodwin's book provides us with the concepts and vocabulary to understand better what we might otherwise only intuitively grasp. This book also forcefully reminds us that as we face a reality that seems increasingly unbearable—climate change, border patrolling, children caged, families ripped apart—Latinx sci-fi urgently matters. It's this space of the Latinx speculative that will open eyes to other ways of imagining and seeing a tomorrow where all of the planet's organic life-forms can discover, create, and thrive in stunning new ways.

Preface: The *X* in the Latinx Files

Although the *X* in Latinx may be challenging to pronounce, it is doing the important work of fashioning a new inclusive language. It is a marker that the structures of language that have been founded in gender discrimination are being realigned. This new usage of *X* embraces multiplicity rather than manifesting worn-out binaries and allows for the undefined and unexplained. The *X* in *The Latinx Files*, which combines Latinx with *The X-Files*, expresses a similar dynamic, that Latinx science fiction is rearranging the structures of science fiction that have not done right by Latinx communities. The space alien in particular is able to express the concerns of Latinx communities, not as the Other but as a Multitude. *The Latinx Files* evokes a fictional television show, in the hopes that Latinx science fiction continues to flourish in print and on the screen, and it demonstrates that space aliens are helping to envision a radically inclusive society.

The Latinx Files

Introduction

■ ■

A Brief Survey of Latinx
Science Fiction

When H. G. Wells published his novel *The War of the Worlds* in 1898, telling of a Martian invasion of Britain, the United States was involved in its own invasion and subsequent colonization of Puerto Rico. The U.S. invasion was less bloody than the Martian invasion, but it has lasted a lot longer, and it has been its own version of a cruel form of colonization. From early on, U.S. officials felt threatened by cultural and language differences. Nelson A. Denis reports in *War against All Puerto Ricans* that in 1902 the Official Language Act made both English and Spanish the official languages of governance in Puerto Rico, and then in 1909 the commissioner of public education, who was appointed by the United States, decreed that speaking Spanish was forbidden in all public schools (41). For a Spanish-speaking nation, this could amount to the decimation of Puerto Rican culture. As Denis describes it, however, the alien invasion was at least partially repelled:

> Then something akin to *The War of the Worlds* occurred. In that novel, Earth is powerless to stop an alien invasion until the humblest creatures, bacteria, destroy the aliens and save mankind from extinction. In a similar fashion, the children of Puerto Rico got fed up with bad report cards and simply stopped going to school. . . . In this manner, children aged six, seven, and eight succeeded where the adults failed. As of 1915, English was still the official language in Puerto Rico's high schools, but Spanish was restored in the grammar schools. (41–42)

In his comparison, Denis places the Americans in the position of the invading space aliens, similar to the way that the novel's narrator places the British in that position. At the same time, Denis takes a creative spin, making use of the bacteria to evocatively represent the powerful children, who after all are just acting naturally in the face of cruelty. These days, of course, the war of words takes place in the media, as children learn both Spanish and English, hybridizing alien influences. I will discuss more about the allegories in *The War of the Worlds* in chapter 1, but here I wanted to give a glimpse of the great potential the space alien has as a rich metaphor. How have Latinx science fiction writers made use of the space alien? *The Latinx Files* is an answer to this question that I have been asking for some years, exploring how Latinx writers are reclaiming this cultural figure that is so often used in a derogatory way to depict people of color, Indigenous groups, and especially immigrants as foreign and threatening. The works discussed in this book show the range of new meanings given to the space alien, and ultimately, the book shows that the space alien has long been significant to Latinx communities.

Before working our way into thinking about the space alien, it is important to get a sense of the general field of Latinx science fiction and the scope of this study. Latinx science fiction, for the purposes of this book, refers to science fiction written by Latinxs living in the United States and should be distinguished from Latin American science fiction. Latin American science fiction, which has a long tradition going back at least to the eighteenth century, has been well charted in the scholarship and there are various studies of the genre's history, in addition to anthologies and bibliographies.[1] Latinx science fiction should also be distinguished from non-Latinx science fiction, which has representations of Latinxs, a study that would certainly merit its own line of research. Latinx science fiction appears in a variety of forms and media, but this book does not examine in any depth Latinx science fiction film, young adult science fiction, or superhero comics.[2] Finally, it is important to note that in terms of classification, the "Latinx" in Latinx science fiction refers primarily to the author's background, not a story's themes. This lack of restriction on the themes is important because it makes clear that Latinx science fiction is not about representing *latinidad* in some specific way, a stance that could have the effect of reducing the perception of what being Latinx in the United States means and arbitrarily forming a restrictive border around Latinx cultures. At the same time, the representation of Latinx characters, cultures, and languages is responsible for much of the vitality of Latinx science fiction. Readers are drawn to these stories in part because of their representation of *latinidad*, and so although the inclusion of Latinx characters or cultures might not define the category, it does influence its reception, who is reading these works, and why. The authors bring the stories to the party, but the stories get the party going.[3]

The initial scholarly essays that dealt specifically with the category of Latinx science fiction had to confront the question as to the history and extent of this subgenre. Emily Maguire's 2012 entry for "Science Fiction" in *The Routledge Companion to Latino/a Literature*, for example, provides a historical outline of the Latinx science fiction tradition beginning with Arthur Tenorio's 1971 novel *Blessing from Above* and ending with Junot Díaz's use of science fiction language in *The Brief Wondrous Life of Oscar Wao* (351–360). The *Oxford Bibliographies Online* 2016 entry for "Latino Science Fiction" by Ilan Stavans and Matthew David Goodwin not only provides a list of Latinx science fiction but also compiles the developing scholarly treatment of Latinx science fiction divided by subgenre. Even with these essays charting the history of the field, there have been continual questions about the extent and impact of Latinx science fiction, as Maguire writes: "few Latino/a names appear in the English-language 'canon' of science fiction writing" (351). Christopher Gonzalez, who notes that science fiction is obviously of interest to Latinxs as evidenced by the great tradition of science fiction in Latin America, poses the question directly: "Why are there so few such [science fiction] works created by Latinos in the United States" (211)? William Orchard also observes: "While Latina/o writers have authored scores of novels in the detective fiction genre, they have produced relatively few science-fiction ones" (649). The general consensus is that there is a thread of Latinx science fiction, although there have been fewer Latinxs writing science fiction than other groups, and that it has not been the most significant genre for the canon of Latinx literature.[4] I generally agree with this consensus, but I do think that the extent of Latinx science fiction and its importance to both Latinx literature and science fiction is larger than is commonly believed and that it is still being recovered. This book is one more step in that process of recovery.

The low numbers of Latinx science fiction novels relative to the wider field of science fiction has compelled numerous scholars to ponder the reason. One piece of the puzzle is to note that the amount of Latinx science fiction in many ways parallels the development of Latinx literature in general, that is, Latinx science fiction has increased over time just as it has taken time for Latinx literature to grow to the enormous corpus that now exists. Frederick Luis Aldama in *The Routledge Concise History of Latino/a Literature* lays out some of the factors that have affected the development of Latinx literature:

> The history of Latino/a literature is the trace-marker of Latinos/as living in time and place as a historical, sociological entity that has become the majority minority population in the U.S. (50-plus million), with a socioeconomic diversity that yields a sufficiently large number of urban-educated, middle-class individuals who, in turn, yield a sufficiently large number of cultural producers, consumers, and interpreters: authors, filmmakers, intellectuals, readers, critics, academics, scientists, and the like. (Preface xv)

The economic and cultural development of Latinx communities is one key piece of the puzzle for why Latinx science fiction has been not so predominant. There is still the point made by Orchard, however, that detective fiction has been more prominent. In other words, there seems to be something specific about science fiction that is affecting this situation. The other key piece of the puzzle of why Latinx science fiction has not been so common is to point to the particular nature of the science fiction community, which has created many challenges for Latinx authors. The science fiction community of writers, readers, publishers, academics, and artists has historically been designed as a White enclave. In *Speculative Blackness: The Future of Race in Science Fiction*, André M. Carrington calls this the "Whiteness of Science Fiction," by which he means the overrepresentation of White people's experiences in science fiction as well as the overrepresentation of White people in the science fiction community (16). Science fiction has outlived other White enclaves in a way only rivaled by institutions such as academia, politics, and country clubs. The White enclave of science fiction is founded in the fact that science fiction arises from and influences thinking about science and technology, and how they will be used in the future. The control of these realms is a form of power that Whites have been insistent on keeping. In this sense, science fiction can be contrasted with magical realism and its ties to fantasy, and detective fiction and its ties to crime, two genres that match the stereotypes of White readers and so have been supported by the publishing industry. Latinx science fiction and its ties to science and technology, however, do not confirm those stereotypes. That the science fiction community is a White enclave does not mean that every person in the imagined community of science fiction is White or directly excludes people or color and Indigenous people, but it does mean that the science fiction community has been an acceptable space for Whiteness to be maintained and expressed. Chicanx science fiction writer Ernest Hogan, in a description of the publication history of his novel *Cortez on Jupiter*, writes: "Everybody in Nueva York back then [1989] just knew that sci-fi was white people stuff.... Once they found out about my Chicanohood, the Nueva York publishing folks tended to act differently. Suddenly, they weren't as relaxed, seemed to be careful about what they said to me (and in front of me)" ("Chicanonauta"). Although the White enclave of science fiction has increasingly been contested, especially of late, it has in no way disappeared. Edward James, coeditor of *The Cambridge Companion to Science Fiction*, describes his reaction to a Latinx character in his entry for the science fiction writer "Sheri S. Tepper" contained in the 2019 encyclopedia *Aliens in Popular Culture*:

> One of the most common images of aliens in popular culture is a cartoon of an alien demanding that an inappropriate person or object should "Take me to your leader." As far as I can discover, only Sheri Tepper (1929–2016) developed

that into a novel: *The Fresco* (2000). The inappropriate person is a middle-aged Hispanic woman from California, and the two aliens appear to her like giant bugs. (262)

It is clear that for James, the idea of a Latinx being a political leader or deeply important to humanity is not just inappropriate but laughably so and cartoonish. This sort of commentary continues as the science fiction community attempts in vain to shore up its walls.

Because of the enormous racism that is connected to the science fiction community, other frameworks have played a vital role in considering works of science fiction in other cultural categories, such as Afrofuturism, speculative fiction, and borderlands science fiction. Ytasha Womack describes Afrofuturism as a category that blurs the borders between genres and takes a critical stance regarding Western science. She writes: "Both an artistic aesthetic and a framework for critical theory, Afrofuturism combines elements of science fiction, historical fiction, speculative fiction, fantasy, Afrocentricity, and magic realism with non-Western beliefs. In some cases, it's a total re-envisioning of the past and speculation about the future rife with cultural critiques" (9). Inspired by Afrofuturism, Catherine Ramírez used the term "Chicanafuturism" in 2004 to examine the futuristic artwork of Marion C. Martinez ("Deus ex Machina"). More recently, Cathryn Merla-Watson (*Oxford Research Encyclopedias* 2019) expands on Ramírez's concept with the category of "Latinofuturism," which is even more expansive regarding themes and communities. In addition to providing a safe intellectual space to discuss multiethnic science fiction, the futurist frameworks provide a way to connect genres and media that are generally studied separately but that share common concerns. Andre M. Carrington expresses the importance of Afrofuturism for Black communities: "This way of positioning science fiction authors as constituents of a Black expressive tradition, rather than viewing them as isolated minorities within a predominantly White community of writers, performs reparation vis-à-vis the alienating effects of the putative Whiteness of science fiction" (24). The positioning of Latinxfuturism performs similar work. Another common framework vital to the scholarly understanding of Latinx science fiction has been the category of speculative fiction, which like Latinxfuturism brings many imaginative genres together in dialogue including science fiction, fantasy, utopian/dystopian fiction, horror, and the like. This framework guided the first anthology of scholarly work on Latinx speculative fiction, *Altermundos: Latin@ Speculative Literature, Film, and Popular Culture* (2017), edited by Cathryn Josefina Merla-Watson and B. V. Olguín, which contains a number of essays on Latinx science fiction. The framework of speculative fiction is particularly helpful in gaining a critical perspective on science fiction that is so bound to Western science. Finally, there is the category of "borderlands science fiction," a subgenre of science fiction designed by Lysa Rivera to show how the colonial context of Latinx science fiction is a defining characteristic ("Future Histories"). The category used in this book, Latinx science fiction, is dependent on and informed by each of these frameworks, all of which share the key quality of wresting the power of future stories away from the White enclave of science fiction and demonstrating how Latinxs are creating new future stories.

As writers, readers, and scholars increasingly use categories such as Latinx-futurism or Latinx science fiction, it is good to remember that there is some cause to walk with caution when using such frameworks. In his essay "Racism and Science Fiction" (2000), Samuel Delany warns against the preoccupation with artificially linking Black science fiction writers together and of creating a Black science fiction tradition separate from the genre itself. The danger in his view is to inadvertently reproduce the separations created by racism. He mentions that even though he is a very different writer from Octavia Butler, he is often asked to speak alongside her at conferences because of the growing interest in Black science fiction (394–396). Even so, Delany does support the effort to recover past works of Black science fiction, one of the purposes of the anthology *Dark Matter: A Century of Speculative Fiction from the African Diaspora* (2000), edited by Sheree R. Thomas, in which his essay appears (383–386). His warning is not a blanket condemnation of the various categories of ethnic science fiction but a cautionary note, a reminder that when you fixate on an ethnic category of literature, you run the risk of perpetuating racism if caution is not taken.

In the case of Latinx science fiction, there are good reasons to at least temporally use the category. We are still in the recovery period of Latinx science fiction, meaning that at least for the present time, there needs to be a focused attention on the group to bring to light works that have not received critical analysis. We need the category to see what has been missed. One of the most important reasons to take up the category of Latinx science fiction is that Latinx writers have been specifically responding to the tradition of science fiction, and they are rearranging that tradition. At the same time, a number of Latinx authors discussed in this book do not identify as being part of the science fiction community but rather the Latinx literature community. In that case, Latinx science fiction is not a racial separator, but a genre division within Latinx literature. Finally, it is good to point out that simply because a story is categorized as Latinx science fiction and is studied in a book about Latinx science fiction does not mean that the story is forever separated from the general category of science fiction or Latinx literature. In fact, many of the works of Latinx science fiction examined in this book appear in traditional science fiction magazines, and others in traditional anthologies of Latinx literature. In this way, Latinx science fiction is better thought of as a lens to see some particular grouping, which can be put on or taken off as needed. At the end of the day though, Delany's warning remains as a constant reminder that the goal of this study is to not separate out Latinx science fiction but to show how Latinx science fiction has been a vital part of both science fiction and Latinx literature all along.

Because the recovery of the historical extent of Latinx science fiction faces a number of challenges, the recovery has taken much effort and it is not the work of one scholar but of many. The first issue involves names. One of the earliest Latinx science fiction authors is the Cuban American writer Luis Senarens, who wrote an influential series of steam-driven robot stories known as the *Frank Reade Library* (1882 to 1898). Like many writers at the time, Senarens used a pseudonym, in his case "Noname" (or, as I like to say, "Noñame") and it was not until much later that the full extent of his involvement was documented.[5] Samuel Delany makes note of this issue in "Racism and Science Fiction":

> I believe I first heard Harlan Ellison make the point that we know of dozens upon dozens of early pulp writers only as names: They conducted their careers entirely by mail—in a field and during an era when pen-names were the rule rather than the exception. Among the "Remmington C. Scotts" and the "Frank P. Joneses" who litter the contents pages of the early pulps, we simply have no way of knowing if one, three, or seven or them—or even many more— were not blacks, Hispanics, women, native Americans, Asians, or whatever. Writing is like that. (384)

Because of the common usage of pseudonyms in early science fiction, it is worthwhile stating that there may be many more Latinx science fiction writers than we know. Beyond the use of pseudonyms, relevant works of Latinx science fiction are often unknown, disregarded, or mislabeled. After Senarens, Latinx science fiction resurfaced in the 1960s. Luis Valdez's short play *Los Vendidos* (1967) is an early work of Latinx science fiction that depicts a group of young Chicanxs who use a robot to trick a representative of then-governor of California Ronald Reagan. Although it is rarely read as an example of science fiction, this play hearkens back to the use of robots to represent class divisions in Karel Čapek's play *R.U.R.* (1920), which coined the term "robot." Another early work is Isabella Rios's *Victuum* (1976), which will be discussed in chapter 5, a novel written entirely through dialogue that recounts the childhood and marriage of Valentina Ballesternos, and her encounter with an enlightened extraterrestrial named Victuum. In this case, the experimental nature of the novel resulted in a very small readership, making it virtually unknown to the wider public and little known to Latinx studies. The influential *Borderlands/La Frontera: The New Mestiza* (1987) by Gloria Anzaldúa, on the other hand, had an enormous readership. As discussed in chapter 2, Anzaldúa not only used the space alien in this work but it played a critical role in her most important theories of cultural mixing and the future. Nevertheless, the science fiction influence on Anzaldúa's work has had very little impact on the enormous wealth of criticism of her work.[6] Finally, Alejandro Morales's cyberpunk-inspired novel *Rag Doll Plagues* (1991) received a good deal of scholarly attention, and yet it was often construed as or mislabeled as magical realism. Even with these challenges, however, the recovery of Latinx science fiction, though slow in coming, has gained great momentum.

Another challenge to the recovery of the history of Latinx science fiction is that telling the history of Latinx science fiction is unlike telling the history of a movement, such as Romanticism, in that there are few definite lines of influence. Isolated moments of inspiration are more common, as is the case with Cherríe Moraga's play *The Hungry Woman: A Mexican Medea* (1995), which is set in the "muy 'Blade Runner-esque'" city of Phoenix after an ethnic civil war has divided the United States into smaller nations (7). To evoke *Bladerunner* (1982) is significant, as it points to two key connections the film has to Chicanx culture. The *Bladerunner* script was written by a Chicanx, Hampton Fancher, who added the character Gaff to the story. Gaff was then played by the Chicanx actor Edward James Olmos, who shortly before the filming of *Bladerunner* had portrayed a classic pachuco in the film *Zoot Suit* (1981), and then developed a futuristic version of this role for *Bladerunner*.[7] Olmos describes his construction of this multiethnic character and the "Cityspeak" he invented to accompany the character as "the culturalization of Los Angeles in a way that people would not be expecting" (*Dangerous Days*). *Bladerunner* has often been seen as depicting the paradigm of the dystopian city; nevertheless, this is the place where Gaff is comfortable and flourishes. Moraga draws on this futuristic setting in her own play to express the complexities of queer Chicanx communities that may appear dystopian to some but that are home to others. What is important to know is that, even if somewhat rare, there are these captivating moments of dialogue in Latinx science fiction history.

If there is one author who represents the entrance of Latinx science fiction into a wider science fiction readership, it would be Ernest Hogan. Even with Hogan's last name, he faced barriers, not only because of the Chicanx themes of his stories but his physical appearance affected his ability to sell books, as he observes: "After my picture appeared in *Science Fiction Age*, I couldn't sell anything anywhere for a few years" ("Chicanonautica"). Hogan's three cyberpunk novels, *Cortez on Jupiter* (1990), *High Aztech* (1992), and *Smoking Mirror Blues* (2001), demonstrated the consistently inventive quality of Hogan's work, such that he is often recognized as a writer vital to the health of Latinx science fiction. In the 2000s, many of the barriers to publishing Latinx science fiction began to erode as a number of mixed-genre novels and short story collections were published that wove science fiction together with other speculative genres.

James Stevens-Arce's novel *Soulsaver* (2000) creates a dystopian Puerto Rico as the setting for a supernatural thriller in which suicides are forcibly resurrected. Sabrina Vourvoulias's novel *Ink* (2012) is set in the near future in which the government has tattooed immigrants. The story is told through multiple perspectives and is written with a mixture of science fiction, fantasy, and mythology. *Latinx Rising: An Anthology of Latinx Science Fiction and Fantasy* (2017, 2020 reprint), edited by Matthew David Goodwin, is a diverse collection that includes some canonical writers such as Ana Castillo and Junot Díaz as well as more up-and-coming authors. Although the Latinx themes of Carmen Maria Machado's short story collection *Her Body and Other Parties: Stories* (2017) are not typically discussed in reviews, it contains some science fiction and has made an enormous impact not only on the speculative fiction community but also the literary world as a whole.

Alongside multiethnic science fiction in general, Latinx science fiction has grown exponentially. There are many more works than can be mentioned here, but the following have been given a good deal of attention. The novel *Lunar Braceros 2125–2148* (2009) by Rosaura Sánchez and Beatrice Pita is structured through the email exchange between a mother and her son, and its vision of worker solidarity has inspired a number of scholarly essays and reviews. Mercurio Rivera's *Across the Event Horizon* (2013) collects some intriguing science fiction stories, including his well-known alien encounter story "Longing for Langalana." A new and inventive *Star Wars* novel, *Last Shot (Star Wars): A Han and Lando Novel* (2018), by the prolific author Daniel José Older, was published in tandem with the film *Solo: A Star Wars Story* (2018). Zoraida Córdova has also contributed to the expansion of the *Star Wars* canon with the story "You Owe Me a Ride" (157–168), which is centered on the bounty hunter Tonnika sisters and was included in *Star Wars: From a Certain Point of View* (2017). Finally, Malka Older has penned a trilogy of cyberpunk novels that reimagined global politics with her Centenal Cycle: *Infomocracy* (2016), *Null States* (2017), and *State Tectonics* (2018). With these more recent works, there is a sense that Latinx science fiction has become a relatively stable field within both science fiction and Latinx literature.

The good news for readers and scholars is that there is more recovering to do and Latinx science fiction is being published at a good pace. Not only will readers and scholars have more of the literature that they love but new topics and critical approaches will emerge. Latinx science fiction is based on the crossing of borders between the two large fields of Latinx studies and science fiction studies, and as these borders are crossed, many possible projects will make themselves known. In fact, this book could not have been written ten years ago, as a number of the stories discussed here were published from 2010 to 2020. I wish to show in this book that the space alien is of particular importance because it has historically been so tied to race and migration, especially the space alien who comes to Earth, which is the focus of this book. Latinxs and Latinx immigrants are often correlated with invading space aliens, and this study demonstrates that Latinx writers have created new space aliens that counteract destructive science fiction narratives and express the concerns of Latinx communities.

In chapter 1, I will deal with the space alien as a general cultural figure and how it has been used in particular ways to shore up the status quo of race and migration. This book argues that Latinx science fiction is reclaiming the space alien, taking it back from its xenophobic and racist legacy, and that it is a vital Latinx figure which is preserving Latinx cultures by activating the myriad possible constructions of the space alien to represent race and migration. The alien reclamation is most powerfully seen in the work of Gloria Anzaldúa, who deeply engages the figure of the space alien and creates a particularly powerful form of alien reclamation, the concept of the alien consciousness that will be examined in chapter 2. In chapter 3, Lalo Alcaraz's work is used to demonstrate the variety of responses to the negative correlation of Latinx migrants with space aliens. In chapters 4 through 6, various iterations of the space alien are explored: the space alien migrant, the enlightened space alien, and the space alien as a source of horror. Each of these demonstrates how Latinx science fiction is reclaiming the space alien in different ways and with new purposes. In chapter 7, I explore the figure of the legendary goat-sucker known as the Chupacabras, and outline my concept of *la conciencia Chupacabras* (the Chupacabras Consciousness), which serves as a counterbalance to Anzaldúa's more optimistic Alien Consciousness. The book concludes with a discussion of the phrase "Fight the Future," contained in *The X-Files* series and how Latinx science fiction has its own form of fighting the future.[8]

One final comment is in order as you open up *The Latinx Files*. The stories examined in this book are written by Latinxs from a variety of cultural and national backgrounds. The largest group represented is Chicanxs, but there are authors with ancestry in Cuba, Puerto Rico, Dominican Republic, Argentina, and Mexico. The space alien is a particularly powerful figure because of its ability to range across these different groups. Precisely because the alien has no nation, no race, no immigration status, and yet at the same time is able to express these issues because of its being a distinct life-form from somewhere else in the universe, it can represent any and all of the diversity within these categories. In that way the space alien is significant for expressing Latinx solidarity, a third space that allows for non-nationalist yet unifying dialogue. But equally important, the space alien is not a utopian figure beyond race and nation—it can just as easily express the tensions and conflicts among Latinx communities through its capacity to express our fears about extraterrestrials. *The Latinx Files* opens a dialogue about the meaning of space aliens in Latinx literature, and seeks the truth about their manifestation in Latinx communities.

1

On Space Aliens

■■■■■■■■■■■■■■■■■■■■■

Scholarly thinking about the space alien is commonly guided by the idea that the space alien is the ultimate "Other." Patricia Monk simply describes the space alien as the "archetype of alterity" (318). Susan Napier complicates the framework somewhat: "The alien is the Other in its most fundamental form, the outsider who simultaneously can be the insider, and it is this polysemic potential that is enthralling and disturbing to the reader" (97). One foundational essay was Ursula Le Guin's "American SF and the Other" from 1975 in which she calls for science fiction to include more sympathetic and more complex representations of the Other with regard to class, race, and gender. The idea behind the space alien as Other is that space aliens are the Other to humanity, and since humanity is a primary identity, the space alien is radically Other. Likewise, space aliens are not from Earth, another of our primary identities. We are humans of Earth, whereas they are nonhumans from space. Most humans, in the words of Dick Solomon from the television show *3rd Rock from the Sun*, are decidedly "galacto-centric" ("Hotel Dick"). Although a person cannot essentially be a space alien, most of us have a tendency to make the category mistake of imagining extraterrestrials as if "they" are space aliens and "we" are the native, human, terrestrials. The space alien conceived as the ultimate Other has another function as part of an allegorical reading of the space alien: it can represent not just one human grouping but any human grouping that is seen as Other in society, such as particular races, classes, sexualities, or even as all Others in a society. The space alien is the ultimate Other because it is constantly being correlated with human Others. As in Le Guin's essay, the framework of the Other is generally used as a critique of certain works of science fiction that are using the space alien in various racist or sexist ways. I think that this common framework of the space alien is useful because the concept can demonstrate that the space alien is often used as a way to dehumanize particular groups of people who are correlated with the space alien. The theoretical framework of The Other is generally tied to particular political perspectives and to the consequences of discrimination. Charles Ramírez Berg writes in his study of Latinx film:

> It is the distortion of the alien immigrant into an Alien Other, and in the case of the Hispanic, the shift from ethnic stereotype to outer-space creature that raises the most distressing set of problems. Some stereotyping researchers have looked at the role of social perception and stereotyping as an important way to understand wide-scale, socially destructive behaviors (on the order of magnitude of genocide, for example, or the Holocaust). (180)

Typically, when the Other is invoked by scholars, the idea is that the space alien is functioning as the Other to the Self of White America. In Ramírez Berg's formulation, the Other is the Hispanic immigrant. To critique this form of othering is a valuable step in working against the cultural influence of racist narratives, but this framework is less helpful in showing how Latinx writers can use the space alien in new ways. The space alien can just as easily represent the Self, that is, it can represent oneself, one's own group, one's race or gender, and not simply in a way that is based on the concept of extreme difference. For example, Gloria Anzaldúa, as will be discussed in chapter 2, relates in an interview her reaction to *Alien*: "The movie *Alien* affected me greatly because I really identified with it. My sympathies were not with the people at all; they were with the alien" ("Spirituality, Sexuality, and the Body" 87). If we think of the alien as the Other, this indicates that we are correlating the Self with the mainstream or with the perspective of a White science fiction author. The space alien framed as Other may be helpful in critiquing Anglo American works of science fiction, but it is not so useful when it comes to the subject of this book, the space alien in Latinx science fiction.[1] This book is about the Latinx reclamation of the space alien, not just the critique of its use by White authors, and this reclamation requires a new framework. The space alien as the Other is the common picture of the space alien, and it has been valuable to many scholars; however, there are good reasons to expand our thinking beyond the idea that the space alien is the Other.

I propose that framing the space alien as a "Multitude" rather than the Other is not only more useful in the particular confines of this book but that it gives us a clearer understanding of the cultural figure of the space alien in general. Debbora Battaglia in *E.T. Culture: Anthropology in Outerspaces* gives some encouragement for what I find to be a more expansive view of the space alien that opens up the possibilities for understanding the space alien as created by Latinx writers. Battaglia writes, "the extraterrestrial . . . 'comes-going' . . . through fields of possible, but in no sense guaranteed, discursive connection" (15). To rephrase this description a bit: *The space alien is a Multitude, existing in a field of possibilities, with many constructions and functions, residing at the intersection of various discourses.* The concept of a field is a key part of this description, because it points to the expansiveness and multiplicity in the space alien's forms and functions. Framing the space alien as a Multitude allows us to observe a broad reclamation of the space alien by Latinx science fiction that embraces the alien in its many forms.

The space alien as a Multitude is seen clearly with an examination of some of the basic aspects of the space alien. No one is a space alien in and of themselves. The concept of the space alien is a relational concept, that is, it is about how one being sees another being. The "alien" part of the space alien is about one being seeing another as different in some way, strange, foreign, and the like. It is not an essential quality, but one that is attributed to another being. At the same time, the space alien is a relative concept. A space alien is an alien from space, that is, a stranger or foreigner from space, and these positions are inherently relative to one's point of view, a point of view that constructs who is alien and who is not. Annette Kuhn describes the situation: "The idea of alien already assumes a point of view: whoever names the alien as such in the very act radically separates herself from it, and it from her" (13). An Earthling meeting a Martian can be just as much of an alien as a Martian meeting an Earthling, and so there is never a solitary space alien. In an alien encounter, everyone is an alien. In addition, the concept of the space alien is mutable, that is, one can be a space alien at one point, but then over time become something else, such as a friend or native. The contextual nature of "alien" in the concept of the space alien is matched by the contextual nature of "space" in the concept of the space alien. Space is also relational, relative, and mutable. Our view of what "space" is will be determined by our relationship to the rest of the universe, and from each position the view of space is always different, and this view is always changing with the expansion of the universe. The space alien is not a fixed figure but a multiplicity of figures, something that is always contextual to the changing nature of relationships and the passage of time.

Another basic aspect of the space alien as a Multitude is simply to acknowledge that there are infinite ways that the space alien can be depicted, that is, space aliens must be constructed as any character in fiction, in terms of their physical attributes, psychological makeup, social organization, linguistic abilities, and so forth. These science fiction constructions can be understood on a scale of increasing alienness from humanity. There have historically been four general sorts of space aliens in fiction: human, humanoid, animal-like, and an overarching category of the radically bizarre. On the low point of the spectrum, space aliens are basically humans, but from somewhere else in the universe. This scenario may be scientifically unlikely, but it provides easy access to the traditional plots of literature. Space aliens are very often depicted as humanoid, that is, as very similar to humans but with some specific differences that provide contrast and narrative tension. Spock from *Star Trek* with his pointy ears and use of extreme logic in a human society that values emotion is a prime example. The third category consists of the aliens who are constructed using the characteristics of animals from Earth, such as octopuses, insects, or lizards. These beings are some of the strangest beings on Earth from a human perspective, and so to give a space alien some tentacles, for example, gives us a small hint, a recognizable standpoint, with which to understand the extremity of the distinction between humans and space aliens. Finally, the fourth category is made of space aliens who are constructed as something completely different, radically bizarre, or unfathomable, such as the conscious ocean of Stanislaw Lem's novel *Solaris* (1961). Often this category includes space aliens who are non-carbon-based lifeforms, or who are simply energy fields. Space aliens in this last category are typically meant to destabilize the all-too-human space aliens so common in science fiction.

Part of my description of the space alien is that it resides at the intersection of various discourses that enter into its field. Some of the predominant discourses are science, science fiction, fantasy, and the paranormal. The background of the cultural figure of the space alien is our own physical universe. As humans explored the universe, we began to be aware of more and more space where there could be living beings. This began with simply looking up at the moon above. Later, our knowledge of the universe expanded as the technology of telescopes developed, and as theories of the universe demonstrated the enormous expanse of the universe with mathematics. This means that many works of science fiction are functioning under the technique of extrapolation (the "what ifs" of science fiction) as they consider what actual space aliens might be like. This has lead science fiction writers to make use of biology and astrobiology, or at least rational speculation, in their constructions of the space alien. The space alien is a science fictional being, that is, an actual possible being in the universe that moves back and forth from science to science fiction. The scientific possibility of the space alien fuels much of the fictional depictions of space aliens, and in that sense, the space alien is unlike giants and fairies. Nevertheless, the space alien has also been historically influenced by folk and fantasy characters. In Lucian of Samosata's second-century travel narrative, *A True History*, the protagonist travels to the moon where he meets all sorts of strange beings such as dog-men. The first space aliens in fiction were conceived as hybrid human-animals, similar to other fantastic travel narratives of the time. Even while they are scientifically possible, space aliens are science fiction fantasies, something that continues in contemporary space alien narratives. Finally, there are many people on the planet who believe that space aliens have come to Earth, and many claim to have had some kind of encounter with space aliens, either by being abducted by them and taken onto a UFO, or by simply meeting an alien and learning from them. Space aliens, like ghosts and angels, are experienced by many people as real beings, even if there is no proof of their existence. It is science, science fiction, fantasy, and the paranormal all woven together that have formed how these fictional beings have appeared throughout history, what they look like, how they live, and what they think of humans.

The multiple discourses crossing through the space alien also results in the space alien being read in various allegorical ways. Allegorical interpretations of the space alien are particularly common because given that the existence of space aliens on Earth has not been verified by science, the space alien in a story does not represent an actual space alien.[2] In addition, there is always something human in the space alien, because when we imagine space aliens, our own human cultures will inevitably form the depiction. Space aliens appearing in fiction and film have been read allegorically to represent all sorts of phenomena. As Heather Hicks notes: "Critical essays have persuasively argued that space aliens have been used to represent communists and homosexuals, along with a host of broader concepts including disease, technology, alienation itself, and even the postmodern problem of truth" (111). Two of the most common allegorical readings, however, connect space aliens to migration and race. These two subjects are deeply tied, and in various ways, to the space alien.

Migration comes into the concept of the space alien through the spatial separation intrinsic to the concept of the space alien. The distance separating life in the universe and that is inherent in the concept of the space alien means that alien narratives imagine at least two worlds, and the distance has to be traversed somehow.[3] At the center of the space alien narrative is a voyage of some kind, a migration between the worlds. The reasons for space migration vary enormously from story to story: exploration, colonialization, invasion, immigration, tourism, university study, political asylum, and so on. Science fiction often emphasizes the actual movement, as is the case with the television show *Battlestar Galactica*, whereas at other times, all that appears is the endpoint, the landing as it were, as is the case with the film *Independence Day* (1996). Aliens travel through space in these narratives, being transformed by and transforming the new worlds they enter.

The space alien who migrates to Earth often is portrayed as having a particular point of view, that of an outside observer who then puts human culture under the microscope as it were. This function appears in the film *The Brother from Another Planet* (1984) directed by John Sayles. The story features a mute three-toed alien ("the brother") who comes to Harlem and faces the challenges that many immigrants face in encountering a new culture. In one scene set in a grocery store, the brother witnesses an exchange of cash for fruit, and he tries to understand why offering bits of green paper to someone will impel them to give you food. What is interesting about this scene is that it is not that he does not understand some common activity such as hailing a cab, but that he does not understand an activity that almost all human immigrants understand. He is an extreme version of a human immigrant. This scene shows that the alien experiences our native world as alien, with the result that the consumer-savvy viewer sees the exchange of money for goods in a kind of abstracted form. Through the meeting of human and space alien, human behaviors, beliefs, and institutions are illuminated.

Race comes into the space alien narrative in a somewhat more complicated manner. On the one hand, race comes in often through migration itself, since the migrant especially in Europe and the United States is commonly racialized. On the other hand, race is not inherent to the concept of the space alien itself, but it does correlate with the relative and relational aspect of the space alien. Race is a relational and relative construct that has the primary consequence of separating out groups of people, that is, race is a form of "categorizing people" (Omi and Winant 105). The space alien works in a similar way and is typically expressed through the different "races" of alien, which have various distinguishing factors such as color. Furthermore, in its most racist expression, race has often been correlated with various biological concepts and has even functioned "as a metonym for 'species'" and therefore correlates with the species difference between humans and space aliens (109). The problem of the depiction of space aliens as racial allegory is that when race is transformed into a stable biological difference between two life-forms without strong references to the history of race, then race is reified and made into a natural difference. In this case, the social and historical creation of race is dropped from the concept. The use of race to construct the space alien renders the figure of the space alien a particularly potent tool because the space alien fixes racial difference as biology and essence. The connection of the discourse of race with the space alien is found in one of the earliest European space alien narratives, Margaret Cavendish's *The Description of a New World, Called the Blazing-World* (1666). In this story, a woman is kidnapped by a merchant and they travel by boat far north. All the men die, but the woman lives and reaches another world through the poles (the blazing world). Along the way to meeting the emperor of this world, she engages the local population: "and as for the ordinary sort of men in that part of the World where the Emperor resided, they were of several Complexions; not white, black, tawny, olive or ash-coloured; but some appear'd of an Azure, some of a deep Purple, some of a Grass-green, some of a Scarlet, some of an Orange-colour, &c" (71). In what is most likely the first example of a "green-skinned" alien in history, the racial element is clearly stated, that is, the races of space aliens are not black, white, and so forth, but blue, green, and so forth. The distinguishing colors directly parallel human races, but since they are in a fantastic world, the colors are equally fantastic. In addition, the essentializing entailed in this alien coloring parallels Cavendish's overt views on race. Cavendish argued in the nonfiction scientific treatise attached to the fictional story that Blacks were not descended from Adam: "Blackmoors [are] a kind or race of men different from the White. . . . For, if there were no differences in their productions, then would not onely all men be exactly like, but all Beasts also; that is, there would be no difference between a Horse and a Cow, a Cow and a Lyon, a Snake and an Oyster" (qtd. in Iyengar 649). In this description, racial difference is comparable to, though not exactly like, species difference. Throughout the history of science fiction, when race-color is evoked by space aliens it is almost always connected in some way to an essentialized vision of racial difference.

The multitude of the space alien and its enormous potential to depict migration and race was constricted by the development of science fiction inside the context of European structures of race and colonialism, and then that of the racial and immigration politics in the United States. The space alien has been put in a cultural straitjacket, and has been from the beginning, as Ziauddin Sardar writes: "Outer space, distant galaxies, the whole universe is populated by fictional creatures intimately familiar from the narrative conventions of Western civilization, springing almost unchanged from the pages of travel literature of the history of Western expansion on planet Earth" (5–6). European exploration and colonization of Africa and the East took a central role in space alien narratives, and writers often turned to the East, China in particular, to construct their aliens. This correlation appeared, for example, in Fontenelle's fictional dialogue, *Conversations on the Plurality of Worlds* (1686), in which the narrator observes: "Look how much the face of nature changes between here and China: other features, other shapes, other customs, and nearly other principles of reasoning. Between here and the Moon the change must be even more considerable" (32). The perceived great divide between the West and East was used to imagine the space alien, and this was just the beginning as various other races and nations became correlated with space aliens.

To understand how the space alien was eventually used in the colonial fantasies of modern science fiction, it is worthwhile to examine one of the most influential of space alien narratives, H. G. Wells's *The War of the Worlds* (1898). The basic idea of the novel is that monstrous Martians have landed in Britain and are killing the population. Although there are numerous literary antecedents that are important to the novel (in particular the genre of invasion literature), the novel's foundation relies on a particular colonial fantasy suggested by Wells's brother Frank, whom Wells credits with having the original idea for the story:

> The book was begotten by a remark of my brother Frank. We were walking together through some particularly peaceful Surrey scenery. "Suppose some

beings from another planet were to drop out of the sky suddenly," said he, "and begin laying about them here!" Perhaps we had been talking of the discovery of Tasmania by the Europeans—a very frightful disaster for the native Tasmanians! I forget. But that was the point of departure. (Qtd. in Fitting 142)

Wells took this basic reversal of European colonialism and formed the novel around it. Throughout the novel, the narrator makes explicit correlations between the invading Martians and the colonizing Europeans. In one comment, he reminds the reader that the Martians are similar to the Europeans and their imperial violence:

And before we judge of them [the Martians] too harshly we must remember what ruthless and utter destruction our own species has wrought, not only upon animals, such as the vanished bison and the dodo, but upon its inferior races. The Tasmanians, in spite of their human likeness, were entirely swept out of existence in a war of extermination waged by European immigrants, in the space of fifty years. Are we such apostles of mercy as to complain if the Martians warred in the same spirit? (Wells 52)

The space aliens are similar to the European colonizers not only because they are more advanced technologically but also because they are destructive and violent. At the heart of the narrator's formulation comparing the Europeans to the space aliens is a typical science fiction reversal. The Europeans, who are in actual life the colonizers, then become the colonized in fiction. As John Rieder describes it: "Wells switches the position of his white Western narrator from its accustomed, dominant, colonizing one to that of the dominated indigenous inhabitant of the colonized land" (7). The principal narrative of the novel is, in fact, a refugee narrative, as the narrator and others flee through the British countryside. The colonizers are reimagined as the sympathetic victims of history, the ones who are conquered because of an encounter with a more technologically advanced group. Wells's reversal, making the colonizer into the colonized, is expressed through an early use of the term "alien" in science fiction, which ironically does not refer to the Martians in the novel: "And we men, the creatures who inhabit this earth, must be to them at least as alien and lowly as are the monkeys and lemurs to us" (Wells 52). The alien is us, from the perspective of the Martians, the extraterrestrials from Earth.

If we further expand the allegorical reversal in which the British are the invaded and colonized, then the Indigenous populations of the world would be the ones invading the British. In this reading, the war of the worlds is an Indigenous or African invasion, a crashing together of "worlds." The correlation between the monstrous aliens and colonized groups is not as explicit as the correlation between the British and the space aliens, and in this way, the story draws on unconscious fears and prejudices. The space aliens are connected to the British by their technology and military invasion, but they are connected to Indigenous groups by the way they are physically described as savage. The Martians, for example, communicate by "hooting," they wear "no clothes," and they have "oily brown skin" (Wells 152, 63). They are also regularly described as having various animal characteristics. The aliens have tentacles, which are compared to snakes, and they are described as being the size of bears, with skin that "glistened like wet leather" (63). In addition, the space aliens, even with their advanced technology, are savage and they drink human blood. The common denominator between the space aliens and the colonized groups is that they are both described by the narrator as being like animals. Recall that in the above quote the "inferior races" are in such a different level of evolution according to the narrator that they are simply the last in a list of animals, like the bison and dodo. Finally, the connection between the space aliens and Indigenous groups is made apparent by the fact that the space aliens are killed by the Earth bacteria to which they are not immune (184). This aspect of the scenario recalls the way that disease was one of the factors in giving advantage to Europeans and Americans in their colonial violence. This correlation between the space aliens and those colonized by the British renders the colonized racial monsters, horrible and nonhuman, sustaining European fears of a postcolonial planet.

The space alien can be a very slippery spot, as different groups slide into the same figure, as is the case here, with the space aliens read allegorically as both the British and Indigenous groups. This creates a certain degree of ambiguity in the novel with regard to its perspective on colonialism. The novel can certainly be read as a critique of colonialism. It seems reasonable to claim that the novel has a kind of literary pedagogy behind it, attempting to teach the British what it would feel like to be colonized. The novel can also be read as a validation of the inevitability of colonization, however, given that the Indigenous groups are depicted as savage. The story should then be seen in light of the Darwinian theories of evolution that are intertwined with the novel and that point toward a naturalizing of colonial invasion. According to the narrator, for example, the violence engendered by this evolutionary gap between Martians and humans is simply the natural order of things: "We men, with our bicycles and road-skates, our Lilienthal soaring-machines, our guns and sticks and so forth, are just in the beginning of the evolution that the Martians have worked out" (Wells 157). The idea is that the situation is, after all, natural, and possibly inevitable, given that the Europeans are superior to what the narrator calls the "inferior races" or Indigenous groups. Nevertheless, the novel can be read either way, as validating or as critiquing colonialism. What is more foundational therefore in understanding how the space alien is being used in the novel is the pattern of reversal on which the ambiguity relies. What is important are the larger ramifications of the reversal itself and the pattern it produces.

My term to describe this narrative pattern, this reversal of the colonizer into the colonized, is the "going alien narrative." The going alien narrative is, more generally, a plot in which an oppressor takes the position of the victim and vice versa. The going alien narrative is the status quo of space alien narratives. I am basing this terminology of the going alien narrative on the "going native" narrative that developed into a full literary genre and cultural phenomenon in the context of colonialism. The typical idea of going native is that a European or American joins with a native group, becoming one with them, experiencing their hardship.

Shari Huhndorf describes in her study *Going Native: Indians in the American Cultural Imagination* the basic role the going native narrative plays in American society: "Throughout the twentieth century, going native has served as an essential means of defining and regenerating racial whiteness and a racially inflected vision of Americanness" (5).[4] She writes that the end result of this sort of narrative is the renewal of European American culture, not Indigenous cultures. While some going native narratives may appear to be sympathetic to Natives, the actual focus is on the White protagonists, as she states: "By adopting Indian ways, the socially alienated character uncovers his 'true' identity and redeems European-American society" (5). In addition, by showing individual Europeans or Americans as peace loving, the going native narrative goes some way toward assuaging White guilt. Huhndorf describes the basic motivation for the going native plot as the "'European Americans' desire to distance themselves from the conquest of Native America" (3). To put it simply, the going native narrative is a White fantasy that is not meant to give agency to Indigenous groups but is meant to take further power from those groups. The going alien narrative functions in a similar way.

At times, the going alien narrative takes the form of a sort of direct "going native" narrative but involving space aliens rather than native groups. In these narratives, the human protagonist is the White man and the Indigenous groups are the space aliens, as in Edgar Rice Burroughs's *A Princess of Mars* (1917). In the novel, Civil War captain John Carter heads out into the American West and ends up in conflict with some Apaches. He hides in a cave and is transported to Mars, where there are "races" of Martians with all sorts of skin colors (red, green, yellow, and so forth). Carter involves himself in the politics of the world, falls in love with a red Martian princess, and becomes the strongest warrior on the planet (due to the advantage he has in an environment with less gravity). Junot Díaz in his introduction to a recent edition of the novel (2012) describes this going alien narrative as a colonial "anti-conquest" narrative in which the hero does not so much conquer the natives as beat them at their own game (xxxi). Other more recent examples of this sort of going alien narrative are the films *Avatar* and *District 9*, which Susana Loza describes similarly as "playing alien" (54). Curtis Marez sums up the general pattern as regards to space aliens: "Representations of alien contact and captivity often enable non-Indians to occupy the position of the oppressed and appropriate the pathos of the victim for whiteness" ("Aliens and Indians" 345).

At other times, the going alien narrative is created not with a specific White protagonist becoming part of alien culture but with the reversal of large categories such as "European" and "Indigenous," as with the case of *The War of the Worlds*. One example is Washington Irving's satirical *A History of New-York from the Beginning of the World to the End of the Dutch Dynasty* (1809), written almost a century before *The War of the Worlds*. This short thought experiment created an even more obvious reversal of powers, as the White Americans took the place of the Native Americans. In this story, moon men, or "lunatics," invade planet Earth, wielding "concentrated sun-beams" (a.k.a. lasers; 83). The lunatics take some of the human leaders back to the moon, finding them strange and savage, and so they put the humans on what are essentially reservations. The human protagonist relates:

> They shall graciously permit us [humans] to exist in the torrid deserts of Arabia, or the frozen regions of Lapland, there to enjoy the blessings of civilization and the charms of lunar philosophy, in much the same manner as the reformed and enlightened savages of this country are kindly suffered to inhabit the inhospitable forests of the north, or the impenetrable wildernesses of South America. (88)

Like *The War of the Worlds*, the going alien narrative here involves the reversal of position and power: the White Americans as victims of the moon people are like the Native Americans who have been victims of the Americans. In some ways, the critique of colonialism is even less ambiguous than that of Wells's critique, and yet the effect is also clearly softened with its obvious satire. Even contemporary scientist Stephen Hawking gets into the going alien game in a Discovery Channel documentary: "'If aliens visit us, the outcome would be much as when Columbus landed in America, which didn't turn out well for the Native Americans. . . . We only have to look at ourselves to see how intelligent life might develop into something we wouldn't want to meet'" (qtd. in "Stephen Hawking Warns"). As with Wells's novel, these examples may certainly be read as a critique of colonialism, or at least a sincere warning, but the pattern and its pervasive effects and ideological limitations remain.

In addition to these variations of the going alien narrative, there is also the capability of the pattern to involve issues other than race, migration, and colonialism, such as gender, sexuality, class, and so on. In this sense, the concept of the going alien narrative is a framework for intersectional analysis. Curtis Marez, in *Farm Worker Futurism: Speculative Technologies of Resistance*, for example, focuses on the category of the farm worker and observes the going alien pattern working in Robert Heinlein's novel *Farmer in the Sky* (1950): "Anticipating a number of similar science fiction narratives, the novel constitutes a sort of race and gender thought experiment that subjects its white male protagonist to conditions experienced by racialized migrant farm workers" (Marez 47). He notes the same pattern in Philip K. Dick's *A Scanner Darkly* (1977), as well as the adapted film, though without the White self-reliant utopianism of Heinlein's novel (Marez 81). The idea is that the going alien narrative is not only the logic of race but of class, gender, and sexuality, and that the power positions can be imagined as reversed to uphold the status quo. The various forms of going alien form a dominant thread throughout science fiction with the result that the kinds of stories being told, who has been telling them, and who gets published has been limited. Examining the going alien narrative throughout the history of science fiction, in fact, is helpful in showing the development of the field, that is, to demonstrate what category the going alien narrative is focused on and how that has changed over time.

It is also important to note that the going alien narrative can be expressed in society at large, not just fiction and film. The figure of the space alien, as a Multitude, is often engaged on a field of battle, on which political debates concerning race and migration are fought. The battles are waged with metaphor and allegory, as various parties jostle to describe what the space alien represents. On one side of the field of battle, the space alien is used to compare immigrants, minorities, or people of color to invading space aliens. This derogatory correlation is typically meant to portray people as foreign and threatening the nation. At times a joke, at other times deadly serious, the correlation is spread throughout the culture in the United States and appears in the form of science fiction narratives, Halloween costumes, T-shirts, and political speeches. Race and migration are constantly intersecting through the figure of the space alien, such as in the continual debate about who the "right" kind of immigrant is and its assumptions about race. In 1882, for example, senator of California John Miller, in a speech promoting the Chinese Exclusion Act, described Chinese immigrants as "inhabitants from another planet . . . of obtuse nerve, but little affected by heat or cold, wiry, sinewy . . . patient, stolid, unemotional [and] herd together like beasts" (qtd. in Huang 95–96). The metaphor is clearly used to dehumanize the Chinese migrants and to portray their presence as an invasion, to describe them as so racially foreign that they are an entirely different life-form, more similar to beasts than humans. The political response to migration is therefore extreme, since from Miller's perspective the Chinese are the racially "wrong" kind of migrants. The Southern Poverty Law Center's *Intelligence Report* recounts that in a 2003 speech, one White supremacist writer described immigrants as "foreign colonizers, like space aliens" (Beirich and Potok, "Paleoconservatives Decry Immigration"). The metaphor of immigrants as space aliens points to the belief that immigrants are racially other, culturally different, and that they are not just immigrating, but taking over. At the same time, White supremacists fear that they are becoming the racial outsiders, the aliens, the strangers living in a new multiethnic land. Their solution is a moratorium on immigration, to build a wall, and close the border to non-White immigrants. This basic going alien rhetoric of immigrant invasion, White victimhood, and an extremist reaction has driven anti-immigrant politics for much of the history of the United States.

The going alien pattern is also present in the very linguistic construction of the space alien. The term "alien" is not neutral in tone; rather, it clearly has had a strong negative connotation. The term's negative connotation can be seen in the sorts of laws that were passed relating to aliens, such as "The Alien and Sedition Acts" (1798), a set of four acts that put restrictions on immigrants deemed dangerous. The term "alien" is also attached to race, as in the 1901 Supreme Court case *Downes vs. Bidwell* in which the phrase "alien race" was used to describe Puerto Ricans as part of the justification for Puerto Rico to remain a possession of the United States rather than an equal partner. This harsh usage of the term "alien" for a foreign national or a foreign race came prior to the use of the term to mean an extraterrestrial. In the nineteenth century, the term was sporadically used to describe someone from another planet, as noted in *The War of the Worlds* (52). Space aliens were featured in literature prior to this, but there is no documented case of them being called aliens. The term gained popularity in the science fiction pulp magazines of the early twentieth century, such as *Amazing Stories*, in which the term is common and is used in multiple ways to describe both alien beings and alien worlds. The negative connotation of the alien immigrant and the alien race was then passed on very directly to the space alien. By this point in history, unless someone has been forced to face immigration law, in which the term is ubiquitous, extraterrestrials come to mind more readily than foreign nationals at the mention of "alien," that is, the most common meaning of aliens is currently space aliens. It is no surprise, then, that a movie can have the title *Alien* (1979) and it is clear that it is about a threatening alien monster, or a movie can have the title *E.T. the Extra-Terrestrial* (1982) and it is equally clear that it is using the term extraterrestrial to distance itself from the invading monster aliens. The term "alien" meaning extraterrestrial seems to have had a backward impact; because people often think of the space alien first now, when immigrants are called "aliens," then people may correlate immigrants with monstrous, or ridiculous, space aliens. The term that already had a negative connotation has now become even more dehumanizing; it emphasizes racial and cultural difference by correlating human migrants with threatening aliens. While the migrant-space-alien correlation is extremely common in popular culture and science fiction, more often than not it conjures a fraught linguistic connection. Although this book most often uses the term "space alien" rather than extraterrestrial, it does so primarily as a way to point to the manner in which the concept of the space alien arises in particular contexts, and more important, to show how Latinx writers are reclaiming the space alien.

Finally, the going alien pattern appears in the experiences that thousands of people believe they have had with space aliens, and there is a distinct going alien sort of narrative working in the abductee community. Certainly the most common image of a space alien—the one that is most often depicted in the television show *The X-Files* and is connected to the UFO landing at Roswell—is the classic gray alien with a large head, small body, and black ovoid eyes. This particular depiction expresses an unusually strong going alien pattern. This alien was popularized through the first mainstream space alien abduction story, that of Betty and Barney Hill who reported that they were kidnapped one night in 1961 driving through the White Mountains in New Hampshire. Under hypnosis, they described what happened to them while being abducted; they both described the aliens as having gray skin (qtd. in Fuller 262, 266, 298). That Barney was Black and Betty was White, during a time when violence against interracial couples was commonplace, certainly played into the experience as well as how others interpreted the experience. They also correlate the aliens with a variety of racial groups: Barney finds them aggressive and thinks of the Irish, who he says are "usually hostile to Negroes" (qtd. in Fuller 90); he says that the aliens look like German Nazis (91); he says they have slanted eyes but not like "Chinese" eyes (92); and he describes them with the facial features of White men though not white skin (124). Betty compares their written language to Japanese (173). The gray alien is an ethnic figure since it is non-White, but it is an ambiguous one since it is gray, and as such, it was appropriated by the abductee community as the iconic space alien. During an age when overt racist depictions of violence are not typically acceptable, this ambiguous image has grown as a hidden cypher of race. The going alien pattern entails that some race or ethnic group is associated with invading space aliens but also important is that Whites take the position of the victim. Some scholars see resonance, for example, in the abduction narrative phenomenon with the genre of captivity narratives in which Europeans and White Americans are kidnapped by Native Americans (see, e.g., Lepselter). According to Christopher Roth, abductees, and the children they claim are hybrid human-aliens, are overwhelmingly White, and with regard to the hybrid children, he writes, "Being an abductee or hybrid is one of the few ways an American WASP can be ethnic" (90). With regard to the hybrid community in particular, he observes, "We can see in this growing movement a co-optation of most of the themes of minority politics" (90). The modern space alien abduction phenomenon is deeply guided by the going alien narrative of White victimhood and monstrous non-White invaders. The going alien pattern is not simply a narrative pattern; it is the logic of race and immigration politics in the United States, as Whites battle for what they perceive to be the moral authority of being the victim.

One of the primary problems of the going alien narrative is that it is a form of appropriation that has benefited the White enclave of science fiction for centuries. Science fiction, in particular the space alien narrative, has great potential to deal with issues of race and migration. From its modern beginnings, however, science fiction has been in part an irrational fantasy that appropriates the experience and oppression of migrants, people of color, and Indigenous groups. Anglo American space alien narratives may be progressive in some ways, but they are not generally Anglo American stories to tell. It is important to clarify that the problem of the going alien narrative is not the reversing of positions of power per se. In fact, such reversals can be profoundly insightful, and in many cases it is clear that White science fiction writers are writing specifically to encourage people to consider the experiences of others. The problem is, like the problem of race in general, the systematic pattern itself, the overwhelming dominance of the going alien narrative. The pattern has created an instability in the field, an inherent contradiction that relies on a romanticizing going alien narrative. One of the reasons that this going alien pattern is so pervasive is that it mirrors the wider phenomena of racism, xenophobia, and other forms of discrimination, which designate some group as an invader and one's own group as the victim of this invasion. In other words, the going alien narrative mirrors the reverse, and perverse, logic of racism and xenophobia itself. The going alien narrative has been so influential because it provides a means for Whites to fantasize that they are on the right side of history.

As the rest of this study shows, Latinx science fiction is offering a font of narratives, alongside multiethnic science fiction in general, that are diverging from the going alien narrative pattern. Latinx science fiction offers different racial and national perspectives, focusing on the experience of Latinxs in the United States, and repurposing science fiction techniques to express those experiences. In doing so, Latinx science fiction is reclaiming the space alien. This does not mean that all of Latinx science fiction diverges from the going alien narrative in all of its forms. It does so typically with regard to the main focus of the book, which is race and migration in Latinx communities. The way Latinx science fiction deals with other multiethnic communities, however, will appear differently in each of the stories discussed in this book, and at times it is clear they can similarly uphold the status quo just as any form of science fiction does. Nevertheless, the appropriation involved in the going alien narrative shows that the Latinx transformation of science fiction is not minor. Latinx science fiction is taking Latinx stories back, and along with postcolonial and multiethnic science fiction, it comes closer to fulfilling the unspoken promise of science fiction made hundreds of years ago—to tell the stories of migrants, people of color, and Indigenous groups.

2

Gloria Anzaldúa and the Making of an Alien Consciousness

■ ■

In *This Bridge Called My Back: Writings by Radical Women of Color* (1981), Gloria Anzaldúa recalls her sense of being different as a child: "The whole time growing up I felt that I was not of this earth. An alien from another planet— I'd been dropped on my mother's lap. But for what purpose?" ("La Prieta" 222). Anzaldúa's statement leaves little doubt about how different she felt, and intimates how people were reacting to her. The metaphor of the space alien is in this case meant to express the extremity of the difference, that is, it was not just that she felt slightly different from those around her, but radically different because of her sexuality, her health issues, and her intense spirituality. At the same time, although she struggled with the radical difference, Anzaldúa connects a "purpose" with the sense of being different. Space aliens don't just appear without reason in a mother's lap, after all. For Anzaldúa, the figure of the space alien expresses a challenge that bears enormous meaning, and she often returned to the space alien in her writings, searching for the radical purpose that lay inside.

In her search for that purpose, Anzaldúa employed the space alien as a "central metaphor" in the manner of her other commonly used metaphors such as the borderland, la Llorona, Coatlicue, or nepantla. For Anzaldúa, a central metaphor is an image that guides a creative work but remains flexible and has multiple meanings that can refer to different aspects or levels of reality, the social and political as well as the spiritual and emotional ("Making Choices" 176).

In an interview with AnaLouise Keating, Anzaldúa expresses her frustration with people using her central metaphor of the borderland as if it had only a specific meaning, "I found that people were using 'Borderlands' in a more limited sense than I had meant it" ("Making Choices" 176). Anzaldúa's use of the space alien in her work comes in part out of her general interest in science fiction, but it is also clear that Anzaldúa sees the great potential in this figure for intersectional and Latinx solidarity.[1]

Each central metaphor has its own affordances, and one of the greatest benefits of the space alien is its inherent multiplicity, as our basic description of the space alien posits: *The space alien is a Multitude, existing in a field of possibilities, with many constructions and functions, residing at the intersection of various discourses.* Anzaldúa activates the multiplicity of the space alien throughout her work to form solidarity, making use of a number of types of space aliens, a plethora of allegorical correlations, and the commonly known and multiple uses of the term "alien." As will be seen, her aliens are characters in her poetry, the beings that humans might encounter one day, and they function to open a field to theorize identity and solidarity. Ultimately, Anzaldúa works through a number of ways of thinking with the space alien as she formulates a vision to express the purpose in the space alien.

One significant alien for Anzaldúa is the monstrous alien from the film *Alien* (1979).[2] In March 1980, Anzaldúa underwent a hysterectomy because of a life-threatening infection, and a month later, she wrote a poem titled "The Alien" (or "Encounter with the Alien"), six versions of which are contained at the Anzaldúa archives.[3] In this unpublished poem, Anzaldúa uses the monstrous alien from *Alien* to express her personal experience with the infection. The narrator, who like Anzaldúa undergoes an operation to take out an infection, describes her entrails bursting out of her body and "crawling on the floor— miles of them / dotted with pulsating mouths like blisters / hot and thirsty with tiny teeth." In another version, it is the "red-veined Alien ~~popping~~ bursting out." The alien not only eats its way through skin but also through steel and concrete. These particular descriptions are similar to the depiction of the alien in *Alien*, which also bursts out of a character in an alien-birthing scene, and whose blood can eat through skin, steel, and concrete. Anzaldúa also plays with the idea that the doctor who is doing the surgery is an alien as well. One version begins: "The knife blade shines in the floodlights. Aliens with white masks hover over me." In this scenario, the doctor is certainly depicted in a threatening way, almost in an alien abduction situation. The aliens in the poem create a reaction of horror and are perceived as a threat, and so it is clear that the narrator is glad that she is being saved. However, there is also the sense that she has not done everything possible to embrace the alien inside her. In one version, she says: "What if I had loved the Alien / looked it in the face / said . . . yes you are a part of me I cannot deny you / I cannot turn my back on you."

The aliens are even given a voice: "You wouldn't look at us. You were too ~~highly evolved~~ proud for the likes of us. . . . Well, you can't turn your back on us. We're flesh of your flesh." The aliens demand recognition not as external invaders, but as a part of her. This aspect of the poem demonstrates a desire to embrace the alien, and shows the psychological difficulty, the guilt, and the horror involved with attempting to do so. The aliens in the poem are never fully embraced, however, and the narrator lives.

As demonstrated in this chapter, Anzaldúa returned to this dynamic of imagining how to embrace the alien in many of her works. For Anzaldúa, the space alien is a measure of one's ability to be inclusive, to embrace that which is unknown or threatening to one's own ego, and this poem gives a sense of those personal limits. The reclamation of the alien is a key to her work as a whole; as Anzaldúa says, "To me spirituality, sexuality, and the body have been about taking back that alien other" ("Spirituality, Sexuality, and the Body" 88). Eventually, as will be discussed in this chapter, the potential to embrace the alien in this poem is developed to the level of not only giving the alien a voice but identifying as an alien consciousness.

In addition to a strong desire to embrace the alien, also significant to Anzaldúa's approach is that she does not simply value the multiplicity of the alien for its own sake but uses it to create new connections among various sorts of being alien, to form solidarity across borders. As Cathryn Merla-Watson observes, Anzaldúa's method of theorizing is a "collective enterprise of suturing multiple constituent elements of identity and lived experience . . ." ("Haunted"). Anzaldúa's suturing of experience and identity is demonstrated in a 1998 interview with Linda Smuckler, in which she explores the monstrous figure of the space alien in the film *Alien*:

> The movie *Alien* affected me greatly because I really identified with it. There was this serpent-like alien being, a parasite, in this man's chest. It exploded; the being rushed out—very much like my out-of-body experience. In the film, it seemed like they were taking all the things they fear and hate about themselves and projecting them onto the monster. Just like we did with blacks and like people do with queers—all the evils get projected. My sympathies were not with the people at all; they were with the alien. I think that's how the soul is: It's treated like an alien because we don't know it. It's like a serpent; it's slimy and bad. That's what they did with women's sexuality and with women. ("Spirituality, Sexuality, and the Body" 87)

In this quote, the fictional space alien creates an open field to bring together the various forms of the alien into a discussion, connecting a variety of issues of discrimination regarding race, sexuality, gender, and spirituality. By connecting these issues, she brings together multiple levels of reality, making clear that the meanings of the space alien is as varied as the borderland, that the concept of the alien works in the physical as well as the spiritual realms. Also finely woven into these connections is Anzaldúa's embracing of the alien as well as her identification and sympathy with each form of alien. The way that the fictional space alien is depicted as a monster in *Alien* definitely does not invite such sympathy, as it positions the human protagonists at the center of the film's point of view. Anzaldúa, however, reads herself into alien, takes the alien point of view, thereby allowing her to see connections that others may not see, and ultimately to express intersectional solidarity through the space alien.[4]

In addition to suturing together the multiple meanings of the alien to form a vision of solidarity, Anzaldúa also emphasizes the radical strangeness of the space alien as a way to express solidarity. The space alien, the migrant from outer space, is often depicted as being radically different from humans, the strangest being humans can imagine. This radicality then offers some further meanings for Anzaldúa to employ. This use of the space alien appears in the following quote, in which Anzaldúa points to the ability of queers to cross cultural borders, thereby serving as a unifying force. She writes in *Borderlands/La Frontera: The New Mestiza* (1987):

> Being the supreme crossers of cultures, homosexuals have strong bonds with the queer white, Black, Asian, Native American, Latino, and with the queer in Italy, Australia and the rest of the planet. We come from all colors, all classes, all races, all time periods. Our role is to link people with each other—the Blacks with Jews with Indians with Asians with whites with extraterrestrials. (106–107)

The term "extraterrestrials" in the above quote is meant to highlight the fact that Anzaldúa is referring specifically to the figure of the space alien, rather than just the "alien" as in a foreign national or the stranger.[5] Anzaldúa is making this distinction because it emphasizes the radical strangeness of the space alien. The idea is that queer sexuality has the capacity to form bonds across various racial groups, and that it has such a powerful potential in this regard that it could even form bonds with the strangest kind of being we could imagine, the space alien. The space alien is the infinite border crosser. Its position as the final item in the list points to this extreme alienness, that is, the space alien is even stranger than Whites, the other contender for a difficult group to form bonds with due to the history of racism. The extent of the unifying potential of queerness is being shown with the mention of the space alien, that is, people of different races can come together through queerness, *hasta los extraterrestres*. The space alien metaphor plays a pivotal role in understanding her vision of solidarity since the space alien is a marker for our capacity to create a radical form of inclusivity. It is also worth noting that the extraterrestrial as last on the list gives the sentence a kind of wry ending, a playfulness that balances what is a pretty optimistic view of the queer capacity to cross any kind of border.

Anzaldúa's use of the more neutral term "extraterrestrial" also leaves open the possible reading that she is not only pointing to the radical strangeness of the space alien but also that she is referring to actual space aliens. The space alien is not just fiction, but science fiction, that is, it is scientifically possible. As Catherine Ramírez observes, the space alien can be read as a literal or metaphorical space alien in this passage ("Cyborg Feminism" 393). This literal reading may seem eccentric to some readers, but Anzaldúa clearly considered the actual space alien. In the interview with Smuckler, for example, she states: "Today our scapegoats are the faggots, lesbians, the third world people, but in the future it will be people from other planets or even artificial humans" ("Spirituality, Sexuality, and the Body" 88). Anzaldúa is imagining in this quote a future time when space aliens have come to Earth and how most humans would not be capable of embracing them. The way the space aliens are functioning in this thought experiment is not only as a metaphor; it is also part of an extrapolation into the future of the dangerous patterns of humanity. If space aliens were to actually show up in the future, humanity would probably continue their habit of finding some group onto which they project unwanted parts of themselves. In this reading of the term "extraterrestrial" as referring to actual space aliens, Anzaldúa considers that should aliens come to Earth, queers, as has been the case throughout history, may be at the vanguard of forming new kinds of relationships.

As seen in the previous example, the space alien can play the role of a speculative concept for Anzaldúa, that is, as a tool for imagining the future of humanity. The space alien as a speculative tool is also expressed in "La conciencia de la mestiza: Towards a New Consciousness," the final chapter of *Borderlands/ La Frontera*, in which Anzaldúa succinctly expresses her fullest expression of the central metaphor of the space alien: "an 'alien' consciousness is presently in the making" (99). With her formulation of the alien consciousness, Anzaldúa imagines that in the future a more evolved humanity will have a more evolved consciousness. This consciousness does not exist in the present moment, but it is in the making. Anzaldúa describes the alien consciousness as a way of being that is tolerant of ambiguity, contradiction, and perplexity, and that does not think dualistically but rather embraces multiplicity. Anzaldúa writes, "She has a plural personality, she operates in a pluralistic mode—nothing is thrust out, the good the bad and the ugly, nothing rejected, nothing abandoned" (*Borderlands/La Frontera* 101). The alien consciousness is radically inclusive, accepting all aspects of oneself and society, and in particular those aspects that are perceived as alien.

As Anzaldúa expresses, the alien consciousness is imagined as arising in the future, but it is also now "in the making," that is, the development of the alien consciousness is an evolution from the present moment. Anzaldúa describes the origins of the alien consciousness as forming in the present-day experience of multiple cultures coming together, as is common in the borderlands. This coming together of cultures results in the psychological challenge of making sense of multiple points of view, conflicting information, and ambivalence. The result for the border dweller is the "swamping of her psychological borders" and "a struggle of flesh, a struggle of borders, an inner war" (*Borderlands/La Frontera* 100–101). To erect walls and boundaries is a response that many people have to this situation; however, this response results in devolution and rigidity, so to move forward, to survive and manage these challenges, the border dweller must be flexible and develop a new consciousness, the alien consciousness. The alien consciousness is based in our human consciousness but it is one that we would hardly recognize because it is the consciousness of humanity in the distant future. It should be clear at this point that the alien consciousness is very much based in Anzaldúa's experience, that it may not be here yet, but there are aspects of it that are present. Anzaldúa sees herself as part of the making of the alien consciousness; she writes, "I am participating in the creation of yet another culture, a new story to explain the world and our participation in it, a new value system with images and symbols that connect us to each other and to the planet" (103). This description of the alien consciousness and how it will arise, however, should not be mistaken for a definition. Anzaldúa offers a variety of descriptions and aspects of her vision of the alien consciousness, but she does not offer such a fixed definition. This indeterminacy is partly a result of this being a speculative construct and therefore indefinite, but more important, Anzaldúa theorizes the alien consciousness similarly to how she theorizes the entire central metaphor of the space alien, that is, as a suturing of identities and lived experiences. The alien consciousness is formed by Anzaldúa not through a definition but through a constellation of ideas and images in a way similar to Leslie Marmon Silko's description of her own theorizing: that it is a "spider's web—with many little threads radiating from a center, crisscrossing each other. . . . the structure will emerge as it is made and you must simply listen and trust, as the Pueblo people do, that meaning will be made" (1575). The form that Anzaldúa's theorizing takes is a mirror to the alien consciousness and its radical inclusivity.

Anzaldúa's particular formulation of the alien consciousness was inspired by the work of Mexican philosopher José Vasconcelos and his speculative theory of *la raza cósmica*. In the section entitled "Mestizaje" of his book *La raza cósmica* (1925; *The Cosmic Race*, 1997), Vasconcelos argues that the many races of humanity will merge together in the future to form a new mixed race, the ultimate mestiza. Anzaldúa initially conceives of the alien consciousness as the form of consciousness of the cosmic race, the way of thinking and being in the world that arises with this new race; that is, going with his outer-spaced themes, a "cosmic" race would have an "alien" consciousness. Anzaldúa directly references Vasconcelos's theory as an inspiration for her concept of the alien consciousness, but she also attempts to avoid some of the shortcomings of *La raza cósmica* (*Borderlands/La Frontera* 99). Vasconcelos's views on race, though influential to the Chicanx civil rights movement for its Brown pride futurism, have been justly criticized. Luis A. Marentes writes that Vasconcelos was "deeply Eurocentric" (103) and that "he has too large an investment in the role of the Spanish—or Latin—peoples for his theory to be a truly cosmic one" (83). His view of a future mixed race, which on the surface is egalitarian, was in fact guided by racial prejudice, as Ilan Stavans describes it:

> "Mestizaje" is an essentialist text that lumps Mexicans, Central Americans, and Latin Americans into a single category without explaining their qualifying differences, as well as a polemical tract that excoriates blacks, Asians, whites, and other ethnic groups. (In later works, Vasconcelos, while condemning Nazism and its orchestration of the Holocaust, became an unrepentant anti-Semite.) (*José Vasconcelos* 5)

Not only does Vasconcelos express a variety of racist views against Indigenous groups and Blacks; his theories of race are quite indefensible, describing the key races too simply as White, Black, "Red," "Yellow" (*José Vasconcelos* 46). In addition, his prediction of a future mixed race involving the coming together of the races amounts to pseudoscience and is based in his interest in Theosophy.[6] Nevertheless, what Anzaldúa takes from Vasconcelos is not so much an essentialist or racist view as the admiration of embracing multiplicity. In a footnote she clarifies, "This is my own 'take off' on José Vasconcelos' idea" (*Borderlands/La Frontera* 119). She characterizes his view this way: "Opposite to the theory of the pure Aryan, and to the policy of racial purity that white America practices, his theory is one of inclusivity" (99). In this way, the alien consciousness is alien not only because it is connected to the cosmic but also because it embraces all that is alien. Taking off from Vasconcelos, Anzaldúa then expands and modifies Vasconcelos's theory, and then weaves it into her own borderlands thinking.

Most prominently, Anzaldúa broadens her focus beyond race, which is signaled by her focus on consciousness rather than *raza*. The alien consciousness, like *la raza cósmica*, involves a mixing and inclusivity, but it does not need to be formed by the mixing of races. This approach is expressed by the multiple names Anzaldúa gives the alien consciousness: "An 'alien' consciousness is presently in the making—a new *mestiza* consciousness, *una conciencia de mujer*. It is a consciousness of the Borderlands" (*Borderlands/La Frontera* 99). The alien consciousness can be formed by the mixing of cultures, sexualities, genders, and so on. Anzaldúa explains her use of the term "new mestiza" in an interview with Jeffner Allen: "I was trying to get away from just thinking in terms of blood—you know, the mestiza as being of mixed blood. The new mestiza is a mixture of all these identities and has the ability, the flexibility, the malleability, the amorphous quality of being able to stretch, and go this way and that way" (qtd. in "Lesbian Wit" 133). Theresa Delgadillo describes Anzaldúa's new mestiza as creating the "possibility for multiple alliances rather than a singular and nationalist embrace of a common heritage," and put another way, Anzaldúa advances "a theory of Chicana subjectivity rooted but not fixed in the experience and epistemology of the U.S.-Mexico border and of queer Chicana feminists" (12, 4). The alien consciousness and *la raza cósmica* are certainly tied together through a correspondence of structure, that is, both involve deep inclusivity, but the alien consciousness is not fixed in the vision of *la raza cósmica*. As Catherine Ramírez describes it: "Anzaldúa does not separate race from sex.... Rather she synthesizes them, along with gender, class, and sexuality into a queer *mestiza* consciousness" ("Cyborg Feminism" 392; emphasis in original). In other words, the alien consciousness is a general approach to intersectional identity, and as such, Anzaldúa describes the alien consciousness in a particularly substantive way: "In attempting to work out a synthesis, the self has added a third element which is greater than the sum of its severed parts" (*Borderlands/La Frontera* 101–102). The alien consciousness is not simply the coming together of cultures or of balancing them; rather, this is an entirely new way of thinking, a new way of living. It is also a vision that science fiction can best convey.

Anzaldúa offers two imaginative depictions of the alien consciousness in two poems included in *Borderlands/La Frontera*: "Don't Give In, *Chicanita*" (her translation of "No se raje, chicanita") and "Interface." The last poem in the collection, "Don't Give In, *Chicanita*," provides a vision of the alien consciousness as based in Vasconcelos's *la raza cosmica*, that is, a depiction of the evolved humans in the future and their alien consciousness. She writes:

> And when the Gringos are gone—
> see how they kill one another—
> here we'll still be like the horned toad and the lizard relics of an earlier age
> survivors of the First Fire Age—*el Quinto Sol.*

> Perhaps we'll be dying of hunger as usual
> but we'll be members of a new species
> skin tone between black and bronze
> second eyelid under the first
> with the power to look at the sun through naked eyes.
> And alive *mi'ijita*, very much alive.

Yes, in a few years or centuries
la Raza will rise up, tongue intact
Carrying the best of all the cultures. (224–225)

This vision of the future has some of the key aspects of *la raza cósmica*. This future human is a "new species" that is a mixture of different races, signified by the dark skin tone; it is also a stronger hybrid culture, taking the "best" of all cultures. Although this future human is an evolved human, not a space alien, it does express the "alien" aspect of the alien consciousness in that it is a different species and has a power that is alien-like, with its second eyelid that enables this human to look at the sun. This ability to look at the sun can be read literally, that like a lizard there was an evolutionary reason for such a development, or it can be read metaphorically as the ability to stare at truth directly, to not hide behind psychological projections, to embrace all. The vision is a political vision of the relationship to the land as well, with gringos gone and the land returned to Mexicans and Indigenous groups.

This aspect is mirrored by the final part of the last chapter of *Borderlands/La Frontera*, in which Anzaldúa writes of her return to the Lower Rio Grande Valley and her awareness of the poverty and the difficulties of farming there. Through the concept of the "Growth, death, decay, birth" of farming, she sutures a vision of the future that ends *Borderlands/La Frontera*:

This land was Mexican once
    was Indian always
        and is.
            And will be again. (113)

This line of speculative poetry is meant to express a firm belief that Anglo control of the borderlands will cease one day. The poem depicting the alien consciousness shows that even though the alien consciousness is not a utopian vision, it still retains a utopian sensibility. Vasconcelos's concept of *la raza cósmica* has an overt utopian element depicting racial unification of the best of all races, and Anzaldúa's alien consciousness retains something of that concept in its hope for radical inclusivity. The alien consciousness can lead to healing, and for Anzaldúa it is the key to a better world: "A massive uprooting of dualistic thinking in the individual and collective consciousnesses is the beginning of a long struggle, but one that could, in our best hopes, bring us to the end of rape, of violence, of war" (*Borderlands/La Frontera* 102). Anzaldúa's direct vision of the alien consciousness contained in "Don't Give In, *Chicanita*" makes clear, however, that the alien consciousness is not a utopian vision per se, as the narrator affirms that there very well may be poverty and violence as in the present. At the same time, the poem expresses the idea that the utopian sensibility of the alien consciousness is vital, as it forms a means to envision the survival and flourishing of Latinx communities in the future.

"Don't Give In, *Chicanita*" is a speculative vision of the alien consciousness as arising from *la raza cósmica*, but Anzaldúa also provides an expanded vision of the alien consciousness with the space alien. This depiction is a vision of the alien consciousness that is not based on race but on consciousness. Anzaldúa took up the fictional space alien in the narrative poem "Interface," which is included in the "Crossers: y otros atravesados" section of *Borderlands/La Frontera* (170–174). This poem is a love story involving a space alien, Leyla, and the unnamed human narrator who lives in New York and has family roots in Texas. The poem describes the development of the romantic relationship between the narrator and Leyla, as well as Leyla's transformation from a nearly invisible alien into human form. At the end of the poem, the narrator recounts bringing Leyla home to Texas at Christmas to meet her family. What is clear about the poem is that Leyla can be read allegorically as referencing any number of the "alien" elements that Anzaldúa references in *Borderlands/La Frontera*, that is, she could be an immigrant, a minority, a Chicanx, the queer, the soul, and so on. All of these are present in the story to a degree, yet none of them is predominant. If we turn our attention to the plot and to the development of Leyla as a character, however, it becomes apparent that the poem expresses the making of the alien consciousness. As such, "Interface" is about employing Anzaldúa's central metaphor in all of its multiple meanings, since the alien consciousness embraces all that is alien.

As in "Don't Give In, *Chicanita*," the being depicted here is an alien consciousness in a quasi-human body. She is an alien-human hybrid, though not one based on race. The development of the plot in "Interface" then mirrors the idea that the alien consciousness is "in the making" (*Borderlands/La Frontera* 99), and the development of Leyla into a humanlike being is a representation of the idea that the alien consciousness is only in the future of humanity, not the present. The story begins with the human and alien on opposite sides of a dimensional border. The scenario is set up so that the narrator inhabits the "physical" world and Leyla inhabits the "noumenal" world, also described as "pulsing color, pure sound, bodiless" (170). Though living in these two distinct realms, they are able to meet briefly in the interface, the border between them. The title "Interface" is significant in this regard, as it is the space between, as well as the point of contact, the point where the narrator can meet her lover, who lives in another dimension. The development of the alien consciousness begins with the alien being present in the world, yet intangible and nearly invisible, but this situation changes. The interface is the promise of a potential birth of the alien consciousness.

Leyla is invisible at the beginning of the story, but as the alien is embraced by the narrator, she becomes visible, historical, and comes out of the closet as it were. In the beginning of the poem, the border is where the narrator can see

Leyla out of the corner of her eye, can pass her hand through Leyla, and they can communicate through telepathy. Eventually, Leyla takes on more substance, leaving traces of a physicality such as the creases on a bedsheet where she was lying. Leyla then takes an important step and becomes more physical, though still intangible "like dense fog" (172). Eventually, the narrator can touch her, and it is at this point that the two—the human and alien—engage in this sex scene:

> A cool tendril pressing between my legs
> entering.
> Her finger, I thought
> but it went on and on.
> I wasn't scared just astonished
>   rain drummed against my spine
>   turned to steam as it rushed through my veins (172)

This beautifully described erotic moment evokes the alien–human abduction commonly depicted in popular culture in which the alien probes the human sexually. It rearranges the meaning, however, to create a moment of sexual awakening. The result for the astonished narrator is that intimacy and pleasure are created in this moment even though the alien does remain strange with her tendril-like fingers. That the story is a love story is important in that it distinguishes Leyla from the figure of the monstrous alien depicted in her poem "The Alien," which was inspired by the film *Alien*. As Anzaldúa makes clear in *Borderlands/La Frontera*, the alien consciousness is also a queer consciousness, embracing all genders, sexualities, and in-between states. This reading connecting Leyla to queerness is strong, given the focus of the story on the romantic and sexual relationship, as well as the direct reference to Leyla being a "lez" at the end of the story (174).

Leyla crossed the border for love, into the physical earthly realm, and the narrator was there to meet her. Leyla then takes full physical and human form through this quasi-birthing scene:

> My roommate thought I was
> having an affair.
> I was "radiant," she said.
> Leyla had begun to swell
> I started hurting a little.
> When I started cramping
> she pushed out
> her fingers, forearm, shoulder.

Then she stood before me,
fragile skin, sinews tender as baby birds
and as transparent. (172–173)

This part of the story has the narrator take the alien into herself, in the powerful embrace of motherhood. This scene is the tipping point for Leyla's development. In being embraced by a mother, the alien is made more public, and
physical as well as spiritual. Leyla is first of all a nontangible state, a pure consciousness, but over time, as the two individuals embrace one another at the
interface, together the two create a "third element which is greater than the sum
of its severed parts" (101–102). The human-alien Leyla is something completely
new, something distinct from both the noumenal alien and the physical human,
and which embraces both. The birth of Leyla is the external manifestation of
the alien consciousness; it is the birth of a new consciousness and it comes with
birth pangs. The narrator is not identified as the alien consciousness. Instead,
she is the mother, the one who gives life to the alien consciousness. This is a
powerful aspect of the poem: the notion that we humans are not now at the
level of being capable of radical inclusivity but that we can strive for it and we
can hope for it.

As the alien consciousness, Leyla now is able to change the world, to super-
humanly change reality—for example, making it snow in the middle of summer, or making the neck of the narrator longer when she wants to reach
something too high. The narrator eventually has to make her stop, and yet the
narrator is curious:

How do you do it, I asked her.
    You do it, too, she said,
my species just does it faster,
    instantly, merely by thinking it. (174)

The idea is that Leyla is reminding the narrator that she too has the power to
change the world. It is not that humans have the potential to change the world;
it is that they already are changing the world. Humans often forget this, however, as they settle into the habits of daily life. It takes an outsider, an alien consciousness, to help us see another way. The alien consciousness is the one that
is capable of bringing about radical change in the world, even to the point that
she could initiate "the end of rape, of violence, of war" (102).

Finally, the narrator takes an important step, bringing Leyla home to meet
the family. This scene is important because it depicts one of the most challenging forms of inclusivity, the most difficult step in the development of the alien
consciousness. The narrator has embraced Leyla, and then her actual mother

embraces Leyla, but what remains as a final obstacle to the complete embracing of the alien are the brothers, the representatives of patriarchy:

Last Christmas I took her home to Texas.
  Mom liked her.
Is she a lez, my brothers asked.
  I said, No, just an alien.
Leyla laughed. (174)

The response given by the narrator is ironic, the joke being that the brothers would find it stranger if she were a lesbian than a space alien. To laugh off a threat can be a form of power, even if it may be the only option one has. Leyla's laughing at the irony of the situation—that she is in fact a space alien—grabs hold of that power and ends the story.

It is important that the ending of the narrative does not show the brothers as changing their minds; in fact, it demonstrates how entrenched they are in their thinking. It finds an inroad, however, a way to unite the brothers into the world of the alien consciousness. They are, after all, family. This sentiment of inclusivity of the intolerant patriarchy through one's own terms is present throughout much of *Borderlands/La Frontera*, as, for example, when Anzaldúa writes: "Chicanos need to acknowledge the political and artistic contributions of their queer. People, listen to what your *jotería* is saying" (107).[7] *Borderlands/La Frontera* is not a book to reject Chicanos, even if it is unflinching in its critique of homophobia in many Chicanx communities. Rather, the book speaks directly to all Chicanxs, showing the way to moments of unification, even if it is over a joke.

The alien consciousness is the conceptual framework that expresses the purpose that Anzaldúa was seeking when she described herself as a child feeling like "an alien from another planet." The alien consciousness embraces that child, and all who are alien in some way. Anzaldúa took her experience of feeling like she was a space alien and transformed it into a speculative concept for radical inclusivity. The fictional space alien as depicted in narratives such as "Interface" are particularly important to the expression of the alien consciousness. Unlike "Don't Give In, *Chicanita*," which does not use the space alien to depict the alien consciousness, "Interface" centers the space alien, and in doing so, it enables Anzaldúa to offer an image of the alien consciousness in the present moment and in a way that does not specifically refer to race. In "Interface," Anzaldúa shows the potential of the space alien to express a powerful form of solidarity that does not rely only on race. The space alien, as a nonhuman entity, can more easily represent any number of races or identities than someone from one particular group. In the work of Anzaldúa, the space alien is a Multitude rather than an Other. The fictional space alien is particularly important for

Latinx solidarity, which Anzaldúa notes has been most often bound to improving representation in the "marketplace" (*Borderlands/La Frontera* 109). She posits, "We need to meet on a broader communal ground" (109). As *The Latinx Files* demonstrates, the space alien is such a broad communal ground, and one that is not specifically correlated with a cultural, linguistic, or racial identity. The alien consciousness is a vision of liberation from racism, sexism, and homophobia, and the space alien is its primary tool. The next three chapters examine how the space alien in other works of Latinx science fiction employ the space alien, in particular in terms of race and migration. At the same time, the space alien has a great capacity to express threats to Latinx communities, which is not a usage that Anzaldúa emphasizes. The use of the space alien as a source of horror will be further discussed in chapters 6 and 7, in particular how the Chupacabras plays a balancing role to the utopian sensibility of the alien consciousness.

3

Reclaiming the
Space Alien

■■■■■■■■■■■■■■■■■■■■■

In 2010, I attended a rally protesting Arizona Senate Bill 1070, a bill that would require police officers to investigate the immigration status of people they suspect of not having immigration documents.[1] A young boy in the crowd held up a sketched homemade poster that contained a picture of a space alien, and the statement "Soy Terrestre, NO ME ARRESTE" (I'm a Terrestrial, DON'T ARREST ME); put another way, "Don't arrest me, I'm not a space alien" (see figure 1). Given the context of the immigration bill being debated, the connection between the immigrant and space alien is certainly working evocatively in the background of this poster, and yet, that connection is immediately disrupted by the declaration of humanity: "I am a terrestrial, an Earthling, a human."

This playful poster can be read a couple of ways. If space aliens are correlated with the immigrant, then it can mean that the protester is not an immigrant. In that case, the poster is correcting a potential case of mistaken identity, that is, the police might suspect that someone is an immigrant because of race or for speaking Spanish even though this would be an unfounded assumption. In this sense, the poster declares: "I'm a citizen, not an undocumented immigrant" and "I may look like I am a foreign national to you, but I'm not an immigrant, so don't arrest me." The poster subtly points to the potential SB1070 has to promote racial profiling of those who are not undocumented immigrants. In another reading, the statement can be read as expressing the primacy of the person's humanity. In this case, whether I am an immigrant or just seem

FIGURE 1 Poster. "Soy Terrestre, NO ME ARRESTE." (Photo by Matthew David Goodwin, 2010.)

foreign to you, I am still a human, and like any human, I have rights. The poster in this sense is a declaration of humanity, that citizen and immigrant both have rights. With these two readings, it is shown how the space alien, as is often the case, has the capacity to refer to both immigration and race at once. It is the metaphorical figure of the alien that makes such a statement of solidarity possible, capable of referencing Latinxs, Latinx immigrants, and Latinxs of any nationality. The ambiguity of the poster engages this complexity and encourages a common political commitment.

In the scenario portended by the poster, the protester is being threatened with an unjust arrest. While the "No Me Arreste" poster rejects the idea that Latinxs or Latinx immigrants are a threat, it has its own idea of what is threatening the nation. The political message of the poster is that the police should not arrest Latinxs and Latinx, like the government arrests the space aliens in films such as *Men in Black* in which space aliens are tightly controlled by the government. In the common correlation that is made between the immigrant and the space alien, the term "alien" is often used as a pun. This correlation is typically a negative one: the people are deemed so foreign that they are like space aliens, or they are seen to be invading like a group of aliens. In the "No Me Arreste" poster, the term "alien" is conspicuously absent; instead, the slogan offers its own play on words: *arreste* and *terrestre*. In addition to being the center of the rhyming scheme in the poster, the primary metaphorical point of contact between Latinxs and the space alien is the experience of being arrested. Because of SB1070, Latinxs—migrants or not—are in danger of being unjustly stopped in the street and arrested because of perceived race or immigration status. The threat the poster names is the police, and by association, the border patrol, and the politicians supporting the bill. In this poster, the metaphor of the space alien is displaced by another central metaphor, that of the men in black and the government authorities who regulate space aliens. They are the real threat, not the space aliens. In spite of the nationwide protests, the main provision of SB1070 regarding police enforcement of immigration law in Arizona has been upheld by the Supreme Court. The anti-immigrant forces largely won this battle, a win that would presage a new and deadly threat, the legitimation of White supremacy and violent xenophobia ushered in with the Trump presidency.

In the "No Me Arreste" poster, one brief burst of political creativity brought science fiction and *latinidad* together to offer a serious repurposing of the science fiction figure of the space alien. Although the poster rejects the idea that immigrants are space aliens, the image on the poster of the classic big-eyed gray alien is not crossed out. It remains present on the poster, and it even seems to be smiling, as if it were in on the joke. The presence of the alien image is part of the poster's playfulness. The poster constructs a new scenario for the figure of the space alien, as it is brought into Latinx spaces rather than being used by the anti-immigrant movement. The poster creators were walking in two worlds as it were: one filled with Latinx concerns about immigration and the other filled with science fiction concepts and images. The coming together of these two worlds, *latinidad* and science fiction, is at the heart of this book.

This chapter lays out some of the specific ways of responding to the particularly negative correlation of the space alien with Latinxs and Latinx immigrants. For these responses, we find inspiration from the graphic artist Lalo Alcaraz, who has possibly more than anyone directly engaged the racist and anti-immigrant correlation of Latinx immigrants with space aliens. In this way, Alcaraz is expressing a key element of the alien consciousness, a reclamation of the space alien that embraces Chicanxs, Latinxs, and immigrants. Through his political cartoons, Alcaraz has produced a wide array of responses in what amounts to a template for the various ways to reclaim the space alien. Born in San Diego to Mexican immigrant parents, Alcaraz has used the figure of the space alien to respond to a variety of political issues, expressing the complexities of contemporary immigration and the varied concerns of Chicanxs. Space aliens feature in all of his major publications, including in his editorial cartoons for the *L.A. Weekly*, which he has drawn since 1992 and which were collected in *Migra Mouse: Political Cartoons on Immigration* (2004). Aliens also appear in his other publications: *Latino USA: A Cartoon History*

(2000), with author Ilan Stavans; *La Cucaracha* (2004), a collection of his nationally syndicated daily series; and *Pocho* (1992–1997), his satirical zine. This chapter will explore six techniques working in Alcaraz's comics that alter the traditional "going alien" narrative that positions Latinx immigrants as invading space aliens and White citizens as victims.

Alcaraz's space alien images come from a variety of sources, but they typically originate in science fiction films or in the popular discourse of space aliens and UFOs. In this way, Alcaraz is able to communicate with a large audience through his political cartoons. Most of Alcaraz's aliens feature space aliens as characters in a Latinx world, such as Spock at the border or E.T. responding to anti-immigrant hysteria. In other cartoons, Alcaraz draws his image in the form of a mock movie poster—creating imaginary Latinx space alien films in an industry in which there are very few. Alcaraz's work can be seen as a first step in addressing this lack. The idea also has precedence in the work of the Chicanx performance group ASCO, who created film still portraits from fictional films, what they called "No Movies." C. Ondine Chavoya and Rita Gonzalez write, "No Movies envision the possibility of Chicanos starring in and producing a wide variety of Hollywood films while simultaneously highlighting their relative invisibility" (Chavoya and Gonzalez 56–57). ASCO created movies with what was available to them. Their "made-do tactics" were then sent out through mail art and were even included in an ASCO-created "No Movie" award ceremony (56–57). Alcaraz uses a similar tactic, but then turns the work away from the art world circuit and into the mainstream popular culture market.

Out of Alcaraz's cartoons we can glean six different techniques that he uses to respond to the racist and xenophobic legacy of science fiction. As will be discussed in the rest of the book, Latinx science fiction writers are also using these techniques. The first technique is the rejection of the idea that Latinx immigration is an invasion. This is a fundamental reaction because when invasion is invoked by the anti-immigrant movement, a strong response typically follows, such as building a wall or increasing deportations. The stakes are high, and it is worthwhile making a clear rejection. The second technique is the classic science fiction reversal, so that while White supremacists may call Latinx immigrants invading space aliens, Alcaraz shows that it is the anti-immigrant movement and the Whites who are more accurately described as the invading space aliens. A third technique is to retain the connection between the space alien and immigrant or Latinx, and yet show that the space alien is in fact a sympathetic figure rather than an invading figure. The fourth technique is to reappropriate the correlation between the immigrant and the invading space alien, but then transform the entire scenario through a Latinx-centered context. The fifth technique is to make use of the space alien as a Multitude to represent various groups and to create a vision of Latinx solidarity. Finally, the sixth technique is when artists or authors depict themselves in graphic art form as a pop culture character—what I call "Graphic Cosplay."

The shorthand I will use for these techniques are—

1 The Rejection of the Invading Space Alien
2 The Threat of the Anti-immigrant Movement
3 The Sympathetic Space Alien
4 The Reappropriation of the Invading Space Alien
5 Space Alien Solidarity
6 Graphic Cosplay

The first technique, the Rejection of the Invading Space Alien, is the most basic response, as it simply rejects the negative correlation between the invading space alien and the immigrant. One of the best examples of this response is the "No Me Arreste" poster discussed above, which explicitly gives the message that "I am not an invading space alien." This first technique runs throughout Alcaraz's political cartoons; I will not be showing a specific one here but will instead point toward it in other examples. This highlights an important point: very often multiple techniques are employed at once, and even play off of one another. The "No Me Arreste" poster expresses an explicit rejection of the derogatory correlation of the space alien with Latinxs, but also uses the second technique as it points to the real threat. As this book shows, however, these two approaches are the tip of the iceberg, because the poster displays only two of the many techniques to use the space alien for political and artistic purposes. Other techniques are ready at hand.

At the base of the second technique is the creation of a reversal in the narrative, changing the norm, or switching around what is real. In a number of images from his zine *Pocho*, which ran in print from 1992 to 1997, Alcaraz makes use of the Threat of the Anti-immigrant Movement technique and correlates the alien invader not with immigrants but with the anti-immigrant movement and former governor of California Pete Wilson. The primary political context for the images is the debate surrounding Proposition 187, a ballot referendum in California that attempted to keep undocumented immigrants from using governmental services, including elementary schools, and would require that any state official report anyone suspected of being undocumented. According to the "Save our State" initiative that sponsored the referendum, "Proposition 187 will be the first giant stride in ultimately ending the ILLEGAL ALIEN invasion" (qtd. in Arnold 409; capitalization in the original). According to the proposition itself, the "People of California" were suffering economic hardship and personal injury because of the "illegal aliens."[2] In addition to being the proposition's most identifiable supporter, Governor Pete Wilson enacted this demand for protection from an invasion by calling out the National Guard to assist the Border Patrol (Massey 89). Meanwhile, Mexican immigrants come to the United States simply to work or to be reunited with their families. Although immigrants were the actual ones on the suffering end of economic exploitation, the law passed in 1994 in the public vote. The law was later deemed unenforceable in federal court and eventually its primary components were repealed.[3]

One image from *Pocho* that involves UFOs is created in the style of a tabloid news article. The image is of Nazis standing around a saucer-shaped ship, and the headline reads: "LOOK OUT, BROWN BOY! HERE COMES PETE WILSON'S PRIVATE FLYING SAUCER!" (capitalization in the original). In the news story below the image, Wilson is described as the leader of a group of "bug-eyed" aliens who are planning on colonizing Earth. They are deporting humans to work in outer space, especially Mexicans, since they "make the best gardeners." The story ends by noting that Caucasians were actually planted on Earth by the aliens as "gringozoid pods" that were meant to wreak "havoc and hell" on Earth. In this work, the Whites, Pete Wilson, and the anti-immigrant movement are the ones who are threatening not only Latinxs but the entire world. At the same time, Alcaraz points to the hypocrisy of Wilson and others who employed undocumented Mexican workers while at the same time working for their deportation. Alcaraz makes the connection between Wilson and invading aliens stronger by correlating the space aliens with Nazis' racist policies. In this instance, Alcaraz is drawing on the conspiracy theory that the Nazis had produced some kind of flying saucer during World War II. Though never confirmed, it has at various times captured the public's imagination as an explanation for UFO sightings. What is important to note is that Alcaraz is creating a science fiction reversal of what is already a fantasy reversal that was made by the anti-immigrant movement. While the anti-immigrant movement positions itself as a victim, Alcaraz places Wilson in the position of the invader, consistent with Wilson's actual militaristic stance. Alcaraz's reverse engineering of the immigrant invader creates a more accurate picture of who is invading and who is being victimized.

In another tabloid image contained in *Pocho*, with the headline "PETE WILSON: SPACE ALIEN!," Wilson is correlated with yet another space alien phenomenon in popular culture, that of the politician as a closeted space alien (capitalization in the original). In this image, Wilson is pictured next to a blowup doll of a space alien with a star-filled cosmos environment in the background. The caption explains that *Pocho Magazine* is presenting "photographic proof" that Wilson is a space alien, noting that the alien next to him is his cousin Mordok, with whom he is discussing "the shortest routes to deportation zones in the outer cosmos." In this image, Alcaraz is making use of this period's particular cultural phenomenon of politicians being "outed" as space aliens in the tabloids (Dean 156). The conceit of newsstand tabloids is that although their claims seem wild and irresponsible, they are offering a truth that is unacceptable in the mainstream.[4] Alcaraz is using this medium to express his own nonmainstream view that it is not immigrants who are invading but Wilson and the anti-immigrant movement.

The Threat of the Anti-Immigrant Movement technique, which changes the anti-immigrant movement or the White supremacist into a threatening space alien, is a common technique used by Alcaraz. With the Sympathetic Space Alien technique, he correlates Latinxs and Latinx immigrants with a sympathetic and noninvading space alien. According to Charles Ramírez Berg in *Latino Images in Film: Stereotypes, Subversion, and Resistance*, one of the developments in the science fiction films of the 1970s was the popularization of films that depicted a sympathetic alien (154). According to Ramírez Berg, "Sympathetic Aliens are allowed to stay if they can offer a unique service to the dominant majority" (167). Some of these films are what he calls "appreciation-deportation" narratives in which the aliens are recognized as sympathetic by some characters and yet are returned to their home planet, as is the case with E.T. (162). Other sympathetic aliens are allowed to stay, but only under the condition that they assimilate into U.S. society, as with the case of Superman (166–167). These films are clearly in the mode of a multicultural ideology, preserving the aliens' strangeness and exoticism while welcoming them with guarded tolerance. Alcaraz has made use of the sympathetic alien on a number of occasions, but instead of using them to express an appreciation–deportation or assimilationist ideology, he uses them to comment on the experiences of Chicanxs and Mexican immigrants.

In 1985, Alcaraz drew a cartoon for the San Diego State school paper *The Daily Aztec* using Spock from the television show *Star Trek* (see figure 2). In this cartoon, Spock has been beaten up by a border patrol officer who apologizes: "Gee, I'm real sorry about that, fellah. . . . I thought you were a <u>Mexican</u>!" (*Migra Mouse* 18, emphasis in the original). One of Spock's pointy ears is bent and one of his arms is in a sling. Nevertheless, he is wide-eyed, the hand of his other arm is clenched in defiance, and he seems to be more ready to take up activism than to pronounce "live long and prosper." The cartoon critiques the brutality that is common at the border by showing that the border patrol officer would beat up someone simply because they are Mexican and before fully recognizing who they are. Alcaraz drew an updated version of this same cartoon in 1994 in which Spock's eyes are squinted to express disappointment and angry resignation (see figure 3). Alcaraz comments on the reproduction, "It just reflects that almost a decade later, brutality at the border still exists" (67).

Another famous sympathetic alien was E.T. from Steven Spielberg's *E.T. the Extra-Terrestrial* (1982). In the same year that *E.T.* marked its twentieth-year anniversary, Alcaraz mirrored this release by having E.T return to

FIGURE 2 Early version of "Dr. Spock at the Border." Lalo Alcaraz, 1984. (Courtesy of Lalo Alcaraz/Andrews McMeel Syndication.)

Earth in his 2002 cartoon "Look! An Alien!" (*Migra Mouse* 106). In the image, a stupid American exclaims: "Look! An ALIEN! He's probably a TERRORIST!" E.T. replies in a thought bubble, "Still no signs of intelligent life," referencing the plot of the film in which the government wanted to sequester E.T. even though he was not a threat (see figure 4). This cartoon expresses a similar idea that Alcaraz had with his two Spock cartoons, that violence against immigrants continues. In this case, what is highlighted is the change in language, since this cartoon is responding to the post-9/11 public hysteria that viewed immigrants as potential terrorists. E.T. was treated badly the first time he came to Earth and he finds a similar problem on his return, just as immigrants have been facing the same ignorance and brutality year after year. The value of the sympathetic alien is that, through its own innocence, it can put into relief this ongoing violence against immigrants, as well as express the exasperation that many feel about the continued injustices at the border.

FIGURE 3 "Dr. Spock at the Border." Lalo Alcaraz, 1994. (Courtesy of Lalo Alcaraz/ Andrews McMeel Syndication.)

Another important element of these two sympathetic space aliens, Spock and E.T., is that while they are sympathetic and not invading Earth, they are not depicted as being cute or cuddly either. They both are shown to have a sarcastic look, and their half-closed eyes are evocative of Alcaraz's comic character Cuco Rocha, who typically wears a wry and perturbed expression. These characters are upset, and liable to protest their conditions. In other words, these are sympathetic and highly intelligent figures, but the cartoons are not meant to convince the viewer of their niceness or goodness. The concept of the immigrant threat often serves as the frame of discussions concerning immigration. Leo Chavez takes on the topic directly in *The Latino Threat* (2008) and argues

FIGURE 4 "Look! An Alien!" Lalo Alcaraz, 2002. (Courtesy of Lalo Alcaraz/Andrews McMeel Syndication.)

that Latinxs are not a threat, that they are assimilating with time, and that the arguments of anti-immigration advocates are without merit. Chavez takes another step, however, to show that immigrants can actively change the nation. To affirm this kind of power that immigrants hold gives them a certain degree of agency; they are creating a new life in a new world. This is an accurate and needed perspective, and one that Alcaraz is able to express in his comics featuring E.T. and Spock.

Alcaraz gives the sympathetic alien a degree of needed agency and activism, but with the next technique he goes further still. The fourth technique used by Alcaraz is the Reappropriation of the Invading Space Alien, which embraces the correlation between the invading space alien and the Latinx immigrant. The idea of reappropriation refers to the situation in which a generally derogatory term or image is repurposed for reasons of empowerment. In a reappropriation, the term or image retains its original form, in this case, the immigrant is depicted as an invading space alien, but the framework is altered. What changes is the use it is put to, the context in which it functions, and its political potential. Alcaraz in fact uses the technique of political reappropriation for a number of potentially derogatory terms. His zine *Pocho*, for example, is named for "pocho," a term that has historically had generally negative connotations referring to Mexicans who have been Americanized. Reclaiming this term is an important move of self-affirmation for Chicanxs. Another term that Alcaraz has reclaimed is *la cucaracha* (cockroach), which is expressed through his character Cuco Rocha. Alcaraz is quoted in the introduction to his collection *La Cucaracha* as saying: "In the U.S., the cockroach was turned into a racial epithet by Americans (who will swear up and down that there is no racism in this country) against Mexicans, Chicanos, and Latinos alike. I reclaim the cucaracha" (qtd. in Harvey 6). It is the use of the invading space alien and its enormous cultural force that has become one of Alcaraz's most significant reappropriations.

One example of Alcaraz's reappropriation of the invading space alien is the political cartoon "S16: Dia de la Independencia" from 1996 in which the aliens are overtly involved in a violent invasion (*Migra Mouse* 84; see figure 5). In this image, an alien spaceship in the shape of a Mexican sombrero shoots a laser down into a Taco Bell restaurant. The cartoon uses the form of the movie poster from the film *Independence Day* (1996) in which a spaceship is blowing up a Los Angeles building (or the White House in another version). The title of this new fictional film, "S16: Dia de la Independencia," refers to Mexican Independence Day on September 16th, and the tag line, "The next time you call them 'aliens' may be your last," expresses the first technique, the Rejection of the Invading Space Alien. Alcaraz is also responding to the hysteria of the citizenry that imagines itself as the victim of foreign colonization. By making the purported invasion of Mexican immigrants into an actual military invasion (with multiple attack sombreros and lasers), the cartoon highlights the hysteria behind this idea and makes a mockery of it.

In this reappropriation of the threatening space alien, Alcaraz rejects the derogatory usage of the space alien, but does not shy away from showing the immigrant as wielding real power. Part of a successful reappropriation is the positive repurposing of the image, moving beyond the critique of previous uses. Juan Poblete writes:

Alcaraz deploys, as it was to be expected, a sharp awareness of the codes and forms of social representation itself. He does so in order to carry out a double semiotic work: first, on the codes of dominant culture for the hegemonic representation of Latinos, and, secondly, on the forms of self-representation of the Latino community. (164)

In this vein, in "S16: Dia de la Independencia" there is an invasion into the Latinx community that is being referenced, the invasion by Taco Bell. We can read this cartoon as depicting a battle scene from what Jose Antonio Burciaga calls "The Great Taco War" in his essay with the same title (21). Taco Bell was founded in Los Angeles in 1962 by Glen Bell, who took the taco he learned about from the Mexican restaurants in the area and adapted it to the

FIGURE 5 "S16: Dia de la Independencia." Lalo Alcaraz, 1996. (Courtesy of Lalo Alcaraz/ Andrews McMeel Syndication.)

American palette by using the ingredients of the traditional American hamburger (Arellano 61–63). In the 1990s, Taco Bell expanded its invasion, brazenly making its way into Mexico City and into the Mission District in San Francisco, both important homes of authentic *taquerias*. In his essay, Burciaga says that he is torn on the issue: "Some hard-shelled Chicanos and Mexicans wouldn't be caught dead in one of these Taco Bells. For others though, an empty stomach and pocketbook do not distinguish the 'real' thing" (25). Although some people may disapprove of the lack of authenticity, the cheap prices draw recent immigrants and the poor. True to his self-description as a "pissed off Chicano cartoonist," Alcaraz imagines a pretty destructive end to Taco Bell with "S16" (*Migra Mouse* 9). But Alcaraz softens his shell through satire, and like Burciaga, puts it all in the context of recent Mexican immigration.

Alcaraz takes another step into a fifth technique, Space Alien Solidarity, which uses the space alien as a Multitude to join groups of people rather than do what the space alien typically does, which is to separate them. The importance of the space alien in the work of Alcaraz is in part due to its wider range than one of his other reclamations, *pocho*, which is very much a part of Mexican culture. While the concerns of "S16: Dia de la Independencia" are clearly based in the experience of Mexicans and Chicanxs, the figure of the space alien can range wider because it can be a nonactual figure on the one hand, and a wide collection of various types on the other hand, and so has the potential to unite Latinxs. There is, of course, always the danger in any conception of solidarity to lean toward the impractical or utopian. Tomás Ybarra-Frausto, in a companion book to a Latinx art exhibit at the Smithsonian, *Our America: The Latino Presence in American Art*, chronicles his practical task of collecting the diversity of Latinx art in the United States. He clearly states that the "concept that Latin American people share a common culture" is "utopian." However, there is still the potential for interaction, as he writes: "Pan-Latino interactions must balance the fantasy of mutuality with the reality of group differences" (15). The space alien, as seen below, can be read as working to affect that balance.

In his 1997 cartoon "Alienated," Alcaraz creates another alien for Latinx solidarity (*Migra Mouse* 81; see figure 6). In this image, a sarcastic alien with a blank expression appears identically in four panels, each with a different caption: (1) "I don't get it. The government denies I exist"; (2) "Hollywood vilifies me"; (3) "Businesses exploit me for profit"; (4) "You'd think I was Latino." The idea is that each of these complaints creatively associates Latinxs with space aliens. The kind of space alien that Alcaraz uses in this cartoon is significant. This is the image of the classic "gray" alien of modern alien lore that is connected to Roswell, Area 51, and alien abduction stories. The first caption, "The government denies I exist," refers to the idea that there is a government conspiracy to hide the existence of aliens and so the government will always deny they exist. The government not only denies Latinxs exist at times, especially with regard to voting districts, but also denies their importance. It has long been a point of protest, for example, that the government has denied social services to Latinxs (as proposed with Proposition 187), in addition to denial of political representation. The second complaint more explicitly equates space aliens with Latinxs, since Hollywood has in fact similarly vilified both of these groups as dangerous threats. The third complaint points to the way that this image of the classic gray alien becomes merchandise, appearing on such things as T-shirts to make money. For Latinxs, the exploitation refers to a wider range of

FIGURE 6 "Alienated." Lalo Alcaraz, 1997. (Courtesy of Lalo Alcaraz/Andrews McMeel Syndication.)

possibilities in the realms of immigrant labor or targeted marketing to Latinxs to make a profit. The important point is that the space alien speaks of "Latinos," indicating that these problems are not faced by some particular nationality but Latinos as a group. This is not a cartoon about immigration or the border, although these elements may be evoked for many viewers, nor is this image about some shared culture of Latin America. Rather, the cartoon highlights how Latinxs are being treated as part of the nation and its institutions.

In 1998, Alcaraz published "Estar Wars," a mock movie poster referencing the movie *Star Wars* in which he uses figures from Latinx popular culture (Mexican, Chicanx, and Puerto Rican) to represent Star Wars characters (*Migra Mouse* 98; see figure 7). Like many of his mock movie posters, this one responds to the publicity surrounding the movie referenced, in this case, to the soon-to-be-released *Star Wars Episode I: The Phantom Menace*, which would be the

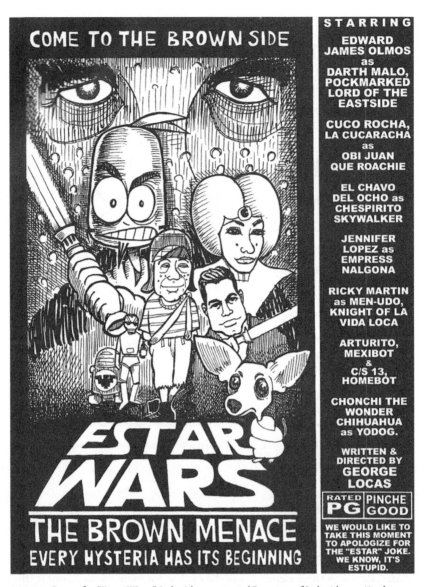

FIGURE 7 Poster for "Estar Wars." Lalo Alcaraz, 1998. (Courtesy of Lalo Alcaraz/Andrews McMeel Syndication.)

chronological beginning of the *Star Wars* franchise. What is immediately apparent about the image is that the figures are all well-known pop culture icons and entertainers who have crossed over the barriers of their own particular national group or heritage and have entered into a more Latinx space. Outside of Puerto Rican communities, Jennifer Lopez and Ricky Martin are seen primarily as "Latin" musicians, and although el Chavo del Ocho is a Mexican character, he became enormously popular throughout the United States, Latin America, and the Caribbean. Even the Taco Bell Chihuahua crosses barriers with his hybrid Mexican American background. Also connected to this wide Latinx space is the invoking of Brown power, as the header reads, "Come to the Brown Side," and the caption under the image reads, "The Brown Menace: Every Hysteria Has Its Beginning." Even the play on words in the title of the work also brings in Spanish, another source of unity among some Latinxs. This movie poster does not offer a utopian vision of shared Latinx culture, however; in fact, the beloved Latinx icons Jennifer Lopez and Edward James Olmos are parodied rather than idolized, and their perceived physical faults are emphasized. Nevertheless, with this work Alcaraz has imagined a full Latinx science fiction film, with Latinxs from a wide variety of nationalities, and with aliens from both the light and dark sides of the force.

Alcaraz's sixth technique, Graphic Cosplay, diverges somewhat from the other five in that its effect is founded on the relationship between the artist and the image. I'm using this term "graphic cosplay" to describe an image in which an artist includes one's own image dressed as, or in the guise of, some fictional character from popular culture. Graphic cosplay is a graphic arts form of cosplay, or costume play, which is most commonly tied to the phenomenon of fan costuming at comic cons. In 2000, Alcaraz created a new mock movie poster entitled "The Mex Files," which is based on the movie poster for the film *Men in Black* (see figure 8). This image combines Mexican culture and American popular culture, along with a DIY aesthetic mixed with mass-produced images. The image uses the bodies of agents J and K from the poster, but they are capped with the cutout heads of Alcaraz and Esteban Zul, his coeditor of *Pocho*. This hybrid image is comparable to a costume that one puts on while remaining somewhat recognizable, often how cosplayers balance their own identity with that of the fictional character, that is, by covering the body and showing the face. The title of the show and the tag line at the bottom also mix in references to the television show *The X-Files*. In addition to the pun in the title, which plays on the common *X* of "Mexican" and *X-Files*, there is the tag line, "The Pochos are out there," which is a variation on the tag line of the opening sequence of the show: "The Truth Is Out There." It is also important that the original title of the film, *Men in Black*, and its overt gender exclusion, as well as the original tag line, "Protecting the Earth from the Scum of the Universe," and its obvious derogatory description of migrants, are left out of this poster. Rather than the sexism and xenophobia of *Men in Black*, the image gives a powerful graphic display of agency, much like Alcaraz's reappropriation of the invading space alien. If these two characters are *pochos* who are also the artists themselves, then their lasers provide them with a great degree of artistic firepower, expressing a politically charged version of "mightier than the sword." Graphic cosplay and cosplay in general are the most direct forms of alien

FIGURE 8 Poster for "The Mex Files." Lalo Alcaraz, 1996. (Courtesy of Lalo Alcaraz/Andrews McMeel Syndication.)

FIGURE 9 *Amor Alien* by Laura Molina, 2004. (Wikimedia Commons cc-by-3.0.)

reclamation, especially when the elements of the characters are consciously modified to express one's own race, gender, and ethnicity. Graphic cosplay is a fan activity, an embracing of a character that expresses that these characters are *our* characters. We perform them because they are ours.

Lalo Alcaraz is not the only artist to engage in graphic cosplay. Chicana artist Laura Molina's painting *Amor Alien*, one of the most recognizable works of Latinx science fiction, is another example (see figure 9). This 2004 painting is a part of the "Naked Dave" series, which was inspired by Molina's relationship with Dave Stevens, creator of the *Rocketeer* comic series. The painting is set on an alien planet with a star-filled cosmos. At the center of the painting is a white man cradling a green-skinned woman in his arms as they rest on a rock. The woman holds a sci-fi caterpillar in her lap and she lies in a somewhat passive state with her eyes closed. The space alien woman, as in other paintings from the Naked Dave series, clearly resembles Molina and the spaceman clearly resembles Stevens. As Molina writes: "The whole idea behind 'Naked Dave' is irony. I could've painted his face onto various scenes of homoeroticism and bestiality but that would be too easy and not very creative. I've deified him as The Cowboy, The Angel, The Greek God so that I may become the iconoclast. (. . . the harder they fall)" ("Dave Stevens: Naked Dave"). The iconoclasm is apparent in two different contexts for the painting. Molina's painting is in part a reworking of the painting *Amor Indio* (c. 1954) by Mexican artist Jesus de la Helguera, whose work often adorns wall calendars. The image in this sense is a parody of the idealized Aztec romances often appearing in Helguera's paintings. This take on *Amor Indio* is made clear by Molina's artist statement, which emphasizes that the relationship ended badly—it was a romance gone wrong. The iconoclasm is also present in the science fiction setting. The green space alien woman in television shows such as *Star Trek* is often the exotic object of interest for white space men. At the same time that Stevens and Molina take these stereotypical roles, however, with Stevens being the protector and Molina the victim, there are these elements that show that he is vulnerable and that she has the actual power. As Robb Hernández observes, on the alien planet, Stevens is the alien—the naked alien—and requires a breathing apparatus, whereas Molina does not (111). This element is made clear by another painting, *The Green Lady*, from 2007, in which the same woman is lying alone as the spaceship takes off into the sky. She is in grief, and Stevens cannot save her, but she is home. In addition, the green woman and her dress are based on the science fiction character Vampirella, and Molina even cosplayed as Vampirella at a convention in 1978: "Vampirella was my favorite comic book character at the time because she was an illegal alien. . . . I appropriated her costume design from Trina Robbins for my Amor Alien painting" ("Vampirella Cosplay"). Vampirella is a powerful space alien, a freewheeling vampire who revels in her conquests, so this connection gives the green woman another degree of power. Molina's image reclaims the green-skinned space alien from its long-distorted legacy in science fiction. Finally, *Amor Alien* is also a kind of reversal of the gender roles in Dave Steven's sci-fi comics such as *Rocketeer*, in which the female lead character is based on the pin-up star Bettie Page who is consistently drawn as a sexual object. In *Amor Alien*, the male character is in that same position. Molina's demonstrates the complex personal and social elements that come together to gain expression in graphic cosplay.

Alcaraz has created a compelling set of political cartoons to deal with the derogatory correlation of the space alien with Latinxs and Latinx immigrants. In terms of rhetorical force, each of the six techniques can be said to have advantages and limitations, and each can be said to draw in different audiences. The Rejection of the Invading Space Alien is the most basic, as it simply though powerfully rejects the correlation given by anti-immigrant Whites. The second technique relies on role reversals, which can be easily recognized and are often aesthetically striking, but they are in many ways politically limiting since they simply offer the opposite perspective on the same situation. The image of the sympathetic alien is an important step and one that allows the work to move away from the anti-immigrant discourse. The fourth technique, the Reappropriation of the Invading Space Alien, does allow for a great deal of expressive range. On the other hand, reappropriation has a decent chance of being misunderstood, or at least read as an ambiguous statement. While the reappropriation of the term "queer" was certainly successful, for example, it is still being used as a derogatory term, as is the space alien as a symbol of immigrants. The risk may be worth it though, if only to avoid romanticized views of immigrants that result in the dissolution of agency. The fifth technique that forms the space alien as a sign of solidarity, especially pan-Latinx solidarity, may be seen as utopian and without connection to the real world where there are real conflicts between groups. As Alcaraz shows through his familiar mockery of aspects of Latinx culture, however, solidarity does not have to be naïve. And finally, Graphic Cosplay has a kind of playfulness that bypasses the more overt political critiques and instead simply reclaims characters that are important to the Latinx community. What is unique in the end is that Alcaraz makes use of all six of the techniques, giving his work a powerful political force that displays the varied perspectives of Latinxs. At this point in *The Latinx Files*, we have not only engaged some important works of Latinx science fiction, but we have also assembled the key elements of a framework for understanding the space alien. Considering the space alien as a Multitude opens up the potential of this figure to be used in ways that are distinct from its racist and xenophobic legacy. Gloria Anzaldúa's speculative vision and Lalo Alcaraz's six techniques show the various ways to then develop those new forms of the space alien. In the upcoming analysis of literature, it is shown through the lenses of Anzaldúa and Alcaraz that Latinx science fiction gives complex roles to the space alien as a migrant, an enlightened being, and a source of horror. Latinx science fiction then expresses the complexities of *latinidad* through the multiplicity of the space alien.

4

Aliens in a Strange Land
■■■■■■■■■■■■■■■■■■■■■

As Lalo Alcaraz shows, there are a variety of possible responses to the derogatory correlation between the migrant and space alien. The short stories examined in this chapter all correlate the space alien with migrants; however, they do so not to show how foreign, strange, invading, or monstrous migrants are, nor how Whites are victims of a migrant invasion. These works extricate the space alien from the "going alien" narrative of science fiction history and demonstrate that it is not the migrant who is the primary threat. These stories make use of the space alien as a Multitude to correlate various groups with the space alien for a variety of political perspectives concerning migrants. With regard to allegorical interpretations, the particular migrant groups that the space aliens are correlated with vary from story to story. With these correlations, the stories express various experiences of traveling to another place and trying to find room for oneself and one's family, of being rejected by society, of living on the outside, of making a life for one's own in spite of the barriers. In each case, the stories use the space alien to depict sympathetic migrant figures who nevertheless are extremely powerful.

Pedro Zagitt's work of flash fiction "Uninformed," from *Latinx Rising: An Anthology of Latinx Science Fiction and Fantasy* (2020), correlates the space alien with the immigrant in an indirect way. The story is set in Queens, New York, on October 30, 1938, at a moment when "the entire island is in chaos because of a radio broadcast" (16). Because the subway is not running, Doña Carmen walks home rather than to the second of her three jobs. Back at home, she comes across a greenish individual she perceives to be an immigrant from Mexico, from Puebla specifically. They have a conversation in which the reader is only given Doña Carmen's side of the conversation, with the other side represented by ellipses. Although she does not understand what the individual is saying, she interprets what he means from such things as his gestures and facial expressions. The gist of the discussion is that Doña Carmen thinks that there is something wrong with the individual, either he is hungry, *empachado* (bloated), or possessed by the devil, and so she offers him lentils to eat and says that she will take him to church. She is insistent, but the individual flees. The narrator ends the story with this phrase: "And without realizing it, Doña Carmen saved humanity from an intergalactic invasion" (17).

The interaction between Doña Carmen and the little green man is first of all comedic and is based on a classic comedic situation of mistaken identity. Doña Carmen believes the individual is an immigrant in need of help and she ponders how to fix his problems. Meanwhile, the space alien is part of an alien invasion of planet Earth. Their purposes could not be more at odds, that is, Doña Carmen is trying to help feed someone who is invading the planet. It is not clear why she does not recognize him as an alien. It could be that the space alien is humanoid to the point that he really could be someone from Mexico, but green. Or it could be that her sight is not so great. At any rate, this is a classic comedic setup. At the same time, the moment when the alien flees at the end of the story is more in the realm of the comedic absurd. It is not clear exactly why the alien flees, but it seems to be a combination of the lentils being so awful, and that the alien experiences the great force of Doña Carmen and what he perceives as her annoying assistance. The reaction of the alien and the defeat of the invading army seem to give Doña Carmen way more power than she has. While it may be an absurdly comedic moment, it is one that expresses some important truths.

In this comedic scenario of mistaken identity, there is a correlation between the space alien and immigrant, though it happens in a particular way. This correlation is formed through dramatic irony, or the literary technique in which the reader believes something different, or knows something more, than a character in the story. In this case, Doña Carmen sees the individual she encounters as a Mexican immigrant, and yet the readers know it is a space alien, since he is described by Doña Carmen as having green skin, and because of the final statement concerning an intergalactic war. Even though readers get much of their information from a one-sided conversation, there is little ambiguity with regard to the actual identity of the little green man. Nevertheless, the means whereby the space alien and the immigrant are correlated is not so much present in the world of the story itself, that is, the space alien is actually not directly correlated with the immigrant. Rather, the correlation is created indirectly through an ironic reading, as the reader negotiates between the two conceptions of who the green man is: the description by the narrator and the description by Doña Carmen.

It should be clear that the indirect correlation between the space alien and the immigrant from Mexico is not an invitation to read this alien allegorically. There is little sense in interpreting the space alien as an immigrant since this alien is an invader. As in the "No Me Arreste" poster discussed in chapter 3, the correlation is there but it is working in the background as it were. Nevertheless, the indirect correlation that is there is not meant to show how strange and foreign the immigrant is, which can be seen by the specific characteristics that Doña Carmen ascribes to the individual whom she sees as an immigrant. She sees him as malnourished and far from home, and it seems to her that he is hexed in some way. She sees him as being in some kind of trouble, but none of this results in him being judged as strange and foreign. On the contrary, Doña Carmen expresses great compassion for him, this immigrant far from home and in need of help.

But while the space alien is not an immigrant from Mexico, Doña Carmen *is* such an immigrant. In this character, we have a direct representation of an immigrant, and one that is largely positive. Doña Carmen is a hard-working immigrant from Mexico who is too busy working to even hear the radio broadcast. She has a store of knowledge that also turns out to be a powerful weapon, capable of repelling an alien invasion. Her weapon is old-school tradition, home remedies, religion, and compassion. It is her sense of solidarity among Latinx immigrants that provides the extra boost of power. She does not even ask the immigrant who he is; she simply sees that he is in need, and proceeds to offer her brand of tough love and care. What seems absurd on one level—that she is able to repel an alien invasion—becomes a means to express the powerful force of a Doña from Mexico who works three jobs and has enough energy to force help upon someone on the street.

There is another element of the story that adds to how readers will understand the story. This detail is the date the action takes place—October 30, 1938—which is also the date that Orson Welles's radio adaptation of H. G. Wells's novel *The War of the Worlds* was broadcast. Welles's show was structured to mimic a real radio show reporting on an alien invasion. Though fictional, it appeared to be a real radio show with reporters, musical interludes, and experts from Princeton. Because of the realism of the show, many people believed that Martians, or some foreign invader, had landed in New Jersey. The sense of impending war in Europe also most certainly fueled the emotional resonance of the broadcast. Newspapers picked up on the story and began describing the event in even more hyperbolic terms as a case of mass hysteria or panic, even though in all likelihood there were a limited number of people who actually panicked to the extent of fleeing their homes (Schwartz, ch. 5). In light of this connection through the date of the events taking place, other aspects of the event come into focus.

The narrative of "Uninformed" includes similar events to those surrounding Welles's radio show. Aliens are featured, and the two stories are also connected by the general scenario that "the entire island is in chaos because of a radio broadcast," but in very different ways (16). Welles's radio broadcast did cause some panic and chaos, but it definitely did not cause the subway lines to stop, and so in the story the chaos seems to be more widespread and stronger. Nevertheless, both stories involve panic and chaos arising from the radio reports of a space alien invasion. In the plots of Welles's radio show and "Uninformed," the alien invasion is real, not fictional. The subject of "Uninformed," however, is not just the plot of alien invasion, but the actual historical reaction of the public to Welles's show. That reaction entailed a public believing to some degree that something false was true. Yet it should be noted that the nature of the radio broadcast in the story, in particular and how it relates to Welles's show, is somewhat ambiguous. That is, the story could be a description of the historical event of Welles's radio show causing a greater panic than it actually did and involving an actual space alien invasion. In this sense, "Uninformed" gives an alternate history of the event, that is, during Welles's fictional broadcast there was, ironically, an actual mass panic and an actual alien invasion happening, which was then derailed by Doña Carmen. Alternatively, the radio broadcast in "Uninformed" could be not Welles's show but an actual news show reporting on the alien invasion—also an instance of irony. In that case, "Uninformed" is a rewriting of the historical moment of Welles's broadcast, an actual alien invasion that happens on the same date as a fictional alien invasion. Fiction and reality are interwoven in this ambiguity. Ultimately, "Uninformed," like the adaptation, offers a strange blurring of fact and fiction, as fictional stories become true and have real effects.

Welles's radio adaptation is, in part, an example of the influence of media and the way that people can be manipulated by propaganda. This emphasis on the media was there in the show itself. At the end of the broadcast, Welles warns: "So goodbye everybody, and remember the terrible lesson you learned tonight. That grinning, glowing, globular invader of your living room is an inhabitant of the pumpkin patch" (Welles 61). Orson Welles takes H. G. Wells's national and racial invading alien and turns it into the media industry, reaching its tentacles into the home. In other words, the real invasion is the incursion of the radio and other media, not postcolonial invaders, into homes. This connection to the media is also present in "Uninformed." One of Doña Carmen's main weapons against the invasion of space aliens is that she is, in fact, uninformed. She has been too busy working to even know what is going on. By ignoring it, she is free of its hysteria. If she had known that the green man was a space alien, she would most likely not have prevailed against the space aliens and the world would have been destroyed. While the media depicts the green man as an invader, just as the media often depicts the immigrant as an invader, she sees him as a compatriot and worthy of care. In this way, and similar to the "No Me Arreste" poster discussed in chapter 3, there is an indirect correlation between the immigrant and space alien, but it is ripped apart at once, in favor of recognizing the human dignity in immigrants.

Unlike "Uninformed," in which the space alien and immigrant are connected but then disconnected, in "Room for Rent" by Richie Narvaez, the connection remains strong and intact throughout the story. "Room for Rent," also included in *Latinx Rising: An Anthology of Latinx Science Fiction and Fantasy* (2020), depicts the aftermath of an alien invasion, with humanity in a subordinate position. Two alien species are present on Earth: the Cangri, who invaded Earth, and who are generally in charge of things, and the Pava, who migrate to Earth to labor in factories. The story is centered on a Pava couple, Hala and Zangano, who are seeking shelter for the impending birth of their children. They rent an apartment filled with vermin, which the reader soon realizes are humans. However, after a visit from a representative of the "Pava Registry and Social Welfare Agency," who notices the presence of vermin in the apartment, one of the humans attacks and kills Zangano. Hala then spears the human with her pincers, and in the tumult Hala's children are born, and they are born hungry.

With regard to the central allegorical interpretation of the story, the Pava can be read as being correlated with Puerto Rican migrants to New York in the mid-twentieth century. The same general scenario is there: coming to a new urban place from a more rural one, dealing with horrible living situations and cruel landlords, and often encountering violence. There is the depiction of migrant nostalgia as well. Sounding like one of the migrant characters from René Marqués's play *La Carreta* (1954), Zangano complains to Hala, "'To be reduced to this,' he said, 'when we once had a home with green all around us'" (108). To expand this allegorical reading, if the Pava are the Puerto Rican migrants, the Cangri are the White landlords, and the humans are something like cockroaches. This reading, as with traditional allegories, is given support by the naming of characters. The name of the species, "Pava," is a type of traditional Puerto Rican hat common in the countryside. Furthermore, the names that Hala gives to the human children are comical Spanish or Spanish-accented terms: Blin Blin, Yerba, and Confley, and the factory manager is Mr. Moco. There is even a Pava rebel faction, which seems comparable to the Puerto Rican Independence Movement, as seen when the representative of the "Pava Registry," who is a Pava but wears a Cangri uniform, questions Hala about her knowledge of the rebel group. Even their physical description, which is in some ways a typical crab-like space alien, connects them to the sea, to the Caribbean. Their animal nature does not so much make them monstrous as give them another layer of a Puerto Rican background. If the Pava can be strongly read as Puerto

Rican migrants, then it is important to explore to what extent they are portrayed as invading or sympathetic space aliens.

The sympathetic nature of the Pavan aliens is in part founded on the point of view of the story, which is in third person but is focalized on Hala and her experience in the new world. Readers certainly might identify with the humans in the story, since readers typically connect to the humans in a story if given the option, but the structure of the story works against this identification. Aside from this narrative element, the typical way science fiction develops space aliens into sympathetic characters is to describe them as somewhat human, with some human characteristics, such that the reader is invited to identify with them. In terms of characterization, the Pavan aliens exhibit characteristics that typically are considered to be emblematic of humanity. Their wants and desires are displayed in the story; in fact, there are few scenarios that produce more sympathy than a poor couple trying to find a good place to have their children. Not only that, but the Pava have what is often considered to be the quintessential human characteristic: empathy. The empathy of the Pava is even biological, as Hala says: "The Pava are empathic, inside. When we ingest another life form, even a dead one, we feel its consciousness, its feelings, its heart" (109). The protagonist Hala in particular is not only empathetic toward what she ingests; she is empathetic toward the humans, who are by all accounts weaker beings. She recognizes first of all that the humans have children, and then goes further to play with them and feed them as if they were her own. It is difficult for many people to imagine feeding the cockroaches in their home rather than spraying them with poison, but such is the nature of Hala's empathy. The Pava may appear to be monsters to the humans, but they do not act as such. Hala, of course, has an ancestor in Frankenstein's monster, another colonial figure who also was depicted physically monstrous to humans yet had a particularly strong sensitivity.

The story also creates a subtle science fiction reversal that results in the space alien being put into the position of the humans. This reversal is based on the distinction between the space alien and human, which is comparable to the distinction between the human and other animals. Animal characteristics are used to construct these aliens' bodies. The Cangri are invertebrates with gray-green flippers, covered in slime, and with eye stems. The Pava are crab-like, with pincers, antennas, and blue blood. It is important to note what kinds of animals are being referenced here; they are not mammals or animals that we generally consider intelligent such as dolphins or monkeys. The humans, in fact, call the Cangri "slugs," which gives a pretty clear idea of what they look like, as well as referencing the fact that a "slug" signifies something base and low (106).

These physical descriptions make the space aliens into beings who are extremely foreign to humanity, that is, they point to the vast difference between human and space alien. The space aliens are as different from humans as humans are from other animals such as snails and slugs. This is also shown by the way the aliens relate to the humans, which is similar to the way humans relate to what many would consider lower animals. In the story, the aliens are generally accepting of killing humans, just as many humans are generally accepting of killing or eating animals such as crabs or slugs. This sense of how distant the aliens are from humanity is also expressed by the use of scientific language in describing the humans, language that would typically be used for animals. For example, the humans are described as having "appendages" rather than arms in the story (104). What all this amounts to is that in the story, the humans are now in the position of the crabs and slugs of the Earth. Meanwhile, the Pava and Cangri, who have the physical characteristics of crabs and slugs, are actually placed in the same position that humans are currently in, that is, in a position in which they have a sense of superiority over lower animals. The Pava and Cangri are the humans of the story, which is a major step toward turning an alien into a sympathetic character.

The Pava are characterized and the story is structured such that the space alien characters, as Puerto Rican migrants, are generally sympathetic figures. The key element, however, that makes space aliens sympathetic is that they are not invading the planet. When the humans realize that they may be exterminated by the Pava Registry, the human leader Fo says through the universal translation device: "<'We know what's happening. You want to kill us. You're just like the slugs.'>" (112). From the perspective of the humans who are being displaced from their apartment, the Pava are just like the Cangri: they are invaders. This leads to the question, Are the Pava migrants or invaders? On the one hand, they are actually taking over the apartment space from the humans. In addition, it is clear that the majority of the Pava see the humans as vermin and are fine with killing them. Although the Pava are highly empathetic, they are not all angelic figures filled with compassion. The other Pava in the story do not show the humans compassion, and Hala herself, once she becomes angry, has little hesitation in having her children eat the humans. On the other hand, the Pava have little choice in where they live or whose apartment they take over. As highlighted by the story title, they are renting a small room, not a mansion. They are the working poor, as Hala works in the Atmosphere factory and Zangano works in the soil factory (in which humans are processed into fertilizer!). Most important, though, is the background on why the Pava have come to Earth. The text says that Hala and Zangano, whose planet was also colonized by the Cangri, were "forced to become laborers" (110). There are few other details about the background, but it seems clear that the Pava came involuntarily to Earth and are at the lower end of the economic system, if not in complete slavery. The Pava, in fact, are like the humans rather than the Cangri in the sense that they are at the mercy of a colonizer. Although there is violence between the Pava and the humans, what the Pava are doing on

Earth is not accurately described as an invasion. If anyone is to blame for the violence and apartment take-over, it is the Cangri who are the actual ones taking over the Earth and setting up a system in which humans and Pava must struggle for even the worst of living conditions. The Pava may be pawns in the Cangri game, but they are not the invaders.

We can explore this question of whether the Pava are invading further by examining a secondary allegorical interpretation in which the plot of the story is correlated with European colonialism. One of the characters, Fo, makes this connection, which is explicit for many readers in the United States. Fo tells Hala the story of the beginning of the Cangri invasion. "They came in three little ships and said they just wanted a place to live. Hah! Soon a few more ships arrived, and then dozens, and then hundreds" (110). Fo's description of the moment of alien contact evokes the three ships of Columbus and the ensuing invasion. Notice that Fo, rather than the story itself, expresses the going alien narrative here, identifying contemporary Americans with Native Americans to prove their innocence. We can work against this way of thinking, however, and use Fo's allegory for another purpose since this double allegorical reading gives another perspective on the question of whether the Pava are invading.[1] In an extrapolation from this colonial description by Fo, the Cangri are the European invaders, the Pava are the African slaves, and the humans are the Indigenous groups of the Americas. We can overlay the Puerto Rican migration allegory on this European colonial invasion. Fo says that the Pava are just like the Cangri, which in this case, would mean that the African slaves are "just like" the invading Europeans. This connection makes little sense, however, especially since that would make the African slaves responsible for the takeover of the Americas (112). Second, we can use the double allegory to show that the Cangri, who are correlated with European colonizers in the colonial allegorical reading, are correlated with the Americans in the Puerto Rican allegorical reading. This puts the Americans in the same position as the Spanish, pointing to the continued colonial status of Puerto Rico under the United States. That the Pava are shown by the story to not be invaders but rather exploited labor, and that Fo is incorrect in correlating the Pava with the Cangri, is important because it shows how the migration of the Pava who came to Earth involuntarily and for economic reasons mirrors the situation of the Puerto Rican workers who migrated to the United States. While "Room for Rent" makes a familiar connection between the space alien and migrant, it does so in such a way as to evoke a dialogue between the past and present colonial scenarios, and affirms that the Puerto Rican migration is not an invasion, but one moment in a larger colonial past.

Brenda Peynado's "The Kite Maker," published at tor.com in August, 2018, like "Room for Rent," retains a strong connection between the space alien and migrant, but in this case, the narrative is not focused on the space alien's perspective; rather, it is focused on the perspective of a liberal-minded human who has very conflicting feelings about the aliens' presence. The story is set in the near future and is centered on the relationship between the narrator, who is a kite shop owner, and a dragonfly-like space alien named Tove Battler of Photons, or just Tove for short. The backstory is that Tove's people came to Earth because their planet, Sadiyada, was on the verge of being engulfed by their sun. They found refuge on planet Earth, but their landing quickly turned into a massacre as the humans were confronted with an alien race for the first time. The humans, including the narrator, physically beat the aliens, many to death, and yet the dragonflies, as they are called by humans, did not fight back. Ultimately, after it was clear that they were not attacking the planet, the humans and aliens found an uneasy balance, and by the time of the setting of the story, they have entered into society. The aliens, however, are clearly the victims of discrimination and they live on one side of town in old warehouses, while the humans live on the other side of town. Neo-Nazis commonly run through the town attacking the aliens as well as the stores that cater to them, and it seems the police are not too helpful. Meanwhile, it turns out that the aliens love kites. Since they cannot fly easily in the heavy gravity of Earth, the kites become a way for them to imagine being free to fly and go back home. The narrator sells her homemade kites to the aliens, and the Nazis burn down her shop as punishment.

The space aliens in this story are quite sympathetic, beginning with the fact that they are bug-like, common enough in science fiction, but they are depicted as being similar to dragonflies, often considered one of the most beautiful of insects. The appearance of the aliens does not seem to immediately evoke revulsion in the humans as in many alien stories, that is, these are not monstrous creatures. They are physically fragile, with two sets of wings, tiny sensitive hairs that cover their bodies, and curving legs. On their home planet, their wings were vibrantly colored, but on Earth they seem to have lost the colored powder on their wings, and so they are brown. Although they are not very strong, they can do precision work with their hands allowing them to make jewelry and clothing. Not only are they physically nonthreatening; they are also culturally nonthreatening. The aliens are generally depicted as shy with the humans, and they do not even have the grammar to make commands in their language, a fact that is matched by how they act, that is, indirectly communicating what they want. If anything, the space aliens are too passive for many humans.

While in "Room for Rent" the Pavan aliens come as exploited labor, the space aliens in this story are refugees who have fled environmental destruction back home. In terms of an allegorical reading, the space aliens are not obviously tied to one particular group. There are a handful of references that give some historical connection to migration. The names of the two aliens, Tove and

Yeshela, and the name of their home planet, Sadiyada, are definitely not common names in the United States. The aliens also have sacred texts that bear great resemblance to the Hebrew Bible, in particular prophecies "about arks, wandering through deserts, how many of them would fall when they got to their new home." Their arrival on the planet is called "The Fallings" by the humans, but they call it "Arkfall." These references together point to the idea that they have experienced something like Noah and his Ark in that they were fleeing a natural disaster to preserve their lives. In this way, the aliens are indirectly connected with Judaism, a group that has been iconic in terms of refugees in the United States. That there is a neo-Nazi group active in the community is also indicative of this correlation. It is also clear, however, that the space aliens are connected to the contemporary discourse about immigrants. For example, their second-class citizen position in society corresponds to that of many immigrants to the United States, and the Earthlings in the story complain of them taking jobs and so on. As has become clear in recent history, neo-Nazis are not just prejudiced against Jews but contemporary Latin American immigrants. Finally, the language of massacres and colonization clearly connect the aliens to Native Americans.

Given this mixture of historical references, while the story can be read allegorically, it can also be read in terms of its extrapolation. What if space aliens such as these were to land on Earth? They would not be entering a vacuum; rather, they would be engaging a society that already has ideas about outsiders. The violence of the extreme Right and the violence of the liberal Left would be a part of that reality. At the heart of the humans' response in the story is the idea that these immigrants are invading, that they are colonizers. The idea first appears in the story with the massacre itself. As the narrator says: "We were sure they were invading, they wanted our children, they wanted more than we could give. We defended our earth." And then later, it is religious leaders who express the more conspiratorial idea of colonization that evokes the arguments made by Europeans against the Indigenous groups of the Americas: "Religious pundits who were horrified at what they'd done tried to justify our cruelty by saying the Dragonflies had no souls. Some of them believed that the aliens were playing a long con, coining the term: There's more than one way to colonize an earth." This phrase, "There's more than one way," is picked up as a chant by the neo-Nazi groups that are attacking the aliens. The neo-Nazis' reaction is the end result of the going alien narrative: that the Whites become the invaders that they fear.

The narrator has a more liberal view of the aliens, although it is a view with a complex background. She does see that they are the victims of discrimination and so perceives them sympathetically. However, the narrator was one of those involved in the massacre, in the beating to death of aliens, and so for her, the aliens induce guilt. At the same time, her views are not just based on some principle of tolerance. She benefits from the aliens in the sense that she is a business owner who makes money off of them. She relies on them economically and so wants to support them. The aliens also make it possible for her to continue to practice her art, since the cultural context is that most people want advanced technology, including her sons, Aleo and Benon, rather than the old-fashioned kites that she makes. The narrator does try to protect the aliens, and even puts herself in danger to protect Tove from the neo-Nazis, but the motivation for these actions is clearly muddled. At the end of the story when the narrator brings an enormous kite to Tove, she realizes her complex emotions about the aliens: "This wasn't charity; this wasn't forgiveness. How could it be, after all that I had done, was still doing? I wanted to fling it in their faces, what they had lost. I wanted to see them hurt for that sky, sing for that lost planet. I wanted them to sing my own song and break open with it." The narrator is a guilt-ridden woman who expresses her guilt by assaulting the dragonflies.

The conflicted emotions that the narrator experiences are manifest in a sexual encounter that she has with Tove. It seems in the story that humans and dragonflies cannot procreate but they can engage one another sexually. The aliens, being so fragile and having sensitive hairs, are turned on by simply blowing air on each other. The narrator actually performs this act on Tove in the backroom of her shop:

> Oh, he said, eyes closing. Oh hemena. His throat buzzed. . . . It was like I was pummeling the words out of him, he said them that painfully. I knew he wanted to say *Stop*. He wanted to say *Desist*. Were those nicknames he had given his fallen mate? Was he trying to call her ghost back across the years? But it was my name I wanted on his purple lips. . . . Benon had never told me what came after, what consummation was for them. Had I known, I would have done it. I know I would have done it.

Though she believes that Tove wants to stop the interaction, she also knows that he will not, and so she takes advantage of him. It is certainly sexual harassment, possibly even rape. The narrator and Tove have both lost their mates, and this connects the two of them in the mind of the narrator. But their intimate moment is forced and aggressive, and only adds another layer of guilt for the narrator.

The space aliens in this story are misunderstood to be colonizers, but in reality they are the victims of both liberal and conservative violence. These aliens also hold a degree of power, however, even if it is positioned as a future power. At the moment when the neo-Nazis are burning down the narrator's shop, the narrator yells at them and says that they are "not fit to inherit the earth." The idea is that the Nazi way of thinking is so outmoded and their ethical and political views so horrible that they should not, and probably will not, be around much longer. They are on the wrong side of history, as the narrator believes. At the same time, the aliens seem to have an idea that they will be staying on Earth for a long time. In response to the narrator's question about why they did not fight when they arrived, Tove says, "You have books that say only the weak will inherit the earth." The narrator then replies, "And if you inherit the earth, what would you do with it?" Tove is silent on this issue. It may be that the aliens end up as the dominant life form on the planet. It also may be that the aliens save humanity one day when the humans have their own environmental collapse, that is, if one of their prophecies comes true, as Benon tells his mother about the aliens' religion: "This is only the third epoch in their religious texts, there's still a fourth and a fifth about going to other places and saving us along with them." This prophecy is clearly not meant to be a declaration of invasion, but it does result in the aliens seeing themselves as surviving the challenges of their present moment and becoming a powerful force in the future of the nation.

Carlos Hernandez's short story "American Moat," contained in Hernandez's collection of speculative fiction, *The Assimilated Cuban's Guide to Quantum Santeria* (2016), is set at the Mexico-United States border and involves a conversation between two militiamen and two space aliens who appear at the border. The two humans, Ham and Alex (short for Hamilton and Alexander), are members of M.O.A.T. (Maintaining Our American Turf), a volunteer militia group that patrols the border. The group seems to be based on the Minuteman Project, an actual extremist nativist border watch group. The action begins as the two men are sitting on their truck, rifles in hand, looking for immigrants, but instead of encountering human immigrants, they encounter two space aliens. These space aliens are ambassadors who have come to Earth to judge the capacity of humanity to join the confederation of planets called the Cosmic Interbrane, which would then allow humanity to access their advanced technology. To demonstrate their powers, one of the aliens turns Alex's truck into Margaret Thatcher. The former prime minister then exhorts the two men to deny entry to the space aliens, even though they are not the typical immigrant "aliens." The two militia men agree to Thatcher's recommendation, resulting in the aliens rejecting Earth's entrance into the confederation. While in "The Kite Maker" the liberal view of immigration is criticized through the figure of the narrator, in this story it is the conservative view of immigration that is criticized through the two militiamen.

The two militiamen are made into somewhat ridiculous stereotypes even while being depicted somewhat sympathetically. Ham, for example, has embraced the silly and short-lived fad of bacon-themed clothing. Alex, by contrast, is more serious, with an actual political philosophy; he reveres Margaret Thatcher as a conservative hero. The two men hate Muslims and want to keep Mexicans out of the country, and they are a sort of Kafkaesque pair of racist doubles who are guarding the border. They are not exactly depicted as evil but as tremendously narrow minded. Ultimately, though, the consequences of their point of view is shown to be disastrous for humanity, that is, the space aliens offer to give humanity the technology to solve the biggest problems that humans face such as poverty, environmental destruction, and war, and yet they reject it based on their racist and anti-immigrant opinions.

The space aliens in the story are entirely under the guise of humans, so the reader does not know their true appearance. They are described as looking "white" and as "a rich couple leaving a Spanish-themed costume ball" (201). The man is dressed in a tuxedo, is "Fred Astaire thin," and his voice is compared to Ricardo Montalban, and the woman is dressed in a flamenco style dress and heels (201–202). At another point they are described by Alex as looking like they were extras "in a Zorro movie" (206). The reader also discovers that the space aliens look the way they do because they are trying to fit in. The aliens have conjured the way they look physically from their limited knowledge of the way people look in that part of the world (which they presumably have learned through television or from the locals' minds). These two Latinx figures in some sense represent the best, most positive, most capable of being accepted figures for racist White Americans. They are exotic and entertaining, they are few not many, and they are European/Spanish rather than Mexican.

As in "Uninformed," this story is initially based on a comedic case of mistaken identity. Ham and Alex believe that the two individuals are Mexican immigrants, whereas they are in fact space aliens. They are confused for being Mexican because they are in the same position, that is, they are requesting entry into the nation at the Mexico–United States border. Ham and Alex come to realize the truth through the aliens' use of telepathy. Nevertheless, there is this initial correlation between the space alien and immigrant. The connection, however, is made with a particular kind of immigrant who is wealthy, extremely intelligent, open-minded, and, we could say, "cosmic-politan." In addition, their mission is essentially political in nature in that they are explorers and ambassadors of the galactic confederation and not looking for a job in the United States. Over the course of their discussion, however, the space aliens become identified with not only wealthy White Spaniards, but with unwanted immigrants. In the discussion between Thatcher and Ham, Thatcher asks them whether they are only stopping Mexicans or other immigrants as well: "'No, not just Mexicans,' Ham added helpfully. 'People from Central and South America and the Caribbean, too. You know, poor people. Who usually speak Spanish. Sometimes French. But not Canadians; they're all right'" (208). The space aliens are not poor and they are White, so that is not the issue. And though they appear to be Latinx and are appearing at the southern border, they are in fact not Latinx.

What, then, is the problem and why do the militiamen deny them entry? The key aspect of the space aliens that makes the militiamen reject them is their legal status. They are requesting entry into the United States without governmental authorization. The space aliens tell the militiamen that they initiate their communication with new planets through its common people, not through an official government entity. This would mean that the duo must allow the aliens in the country themselves, thereby breaking U.S. immigration laws (they do not, of course, consider the fact that, technically, immigration laws would apply only to humans). At Thatcher's prodding, Alex comes to the following conclusion: "Our sole mandate is to keep unauthorized aliens out. And right now, these two are unauthorized. Illegal" (208). This stance indicates an extreme rigidity of thinking, and it is to the detriment of humanity. The other reason that the aliens are denied entry is that if the humans are accepted into the Cosmic Interbrane, then Earth's governmental bodies will no longer have authority. Humanity will join the Cosmic Interbrane and be citizens of that governing body. Thatcher, Alex, and Ham are all obvious nationalists, and even more so, they support the global system of nations and its concomitant regulation of migration.

Opposed to the rigid views of Ham and Alex is the view of the space aliens. They are offering a lot: world peace, all human needs met, the ability to manipulate matter, the end of environmental destruction, the ability to travel through the universe, telepathy. This is a major development for humanity, and on the surface at least, will be of great benefit to humanity. This scenario that will result in the dissipation of human governance would cause many people to hesitate. However, this is exactly the point of view that is being offered: a larger, nonprovincial perspective on the universe. As the alien woman says, "'Our arrival will begin a new evolutionary stage for humanity'" (206). Humans have the chance to take the next evolutionary step, possibly one that will save humanity from destroying itself and the planet. Ham and Alex, however, are tied to their nationalistic viewpoint that they need to protect their nation from changing. In contrast, the aliens have a higher viewpoint, one that is beyond the confines of nationalism. Indeed, the Cosmic Interbrane can be easily read as a metaphor for the United Nations. This larger viewpoint is, in fact, a common one that is connected to space aliens because once humans meet space aliens, our differences pale in comparison to the differences between humans and aliens. But in this story, that larger viewpoint is not actualized; it is rejected, just as it is by the anti-immigrant movement. "American Moat" tells a story about the modern tragicomedy that is the present-day United States, turning its back on its own history of immigration.

Some of the stories discussed in this chapter are humorous, others are more serious, but they all prominently use the third technique described in chapter 3, the Sympathetic Space Alien, to diverge from the racist and anti-immigrant legacy of the invading space alien. This is a basic yet key step in the development of the alien consciousness, as the immigrant as threat trope will always evoke separation rather than embracing multiplicity. The motivations for the migrations in large part makes the immigrants sympathetic, that is, they come not to invade and kill humans. Rather, they come because of some sort of hardship, or they have some intention to help humanity, or they may even come involuntarily. Given the history of space aliens in science fiction, the use of the Sympathetic Space Alien is not surprising, as this figure has the potential to most clearly oppose that legacy with a positive alternative. Even so, as in Alcaraz's work, the sympathetic migrant characters in these stories nevertheless have a good deal of agency. They are not invading but have the potential to change the status quo and transform the nation.

5

The Unbearable
Enlightenment of the
Space Alien

■ ■

It is not always useful to read the space alien as an allegory of race and migration. At times, it is important to recognize the other uses, functions, and depictions of the space alien. In this chapter, we explore the figure of the space alien as an enlightened being. In this sense, the space alien functions more as an extrapolation, as authors speculate about what space aliens might be like based on what we know. In the scenario of aliens coming to Earth or to our solar system, it can be safely assumed that the aliens have progressed beyond the current state of science on Earth so that they are able to travel at the speeds necessary to reach Earth from across space. Latinx science fiction makes use of this speculation about the space alien to express not only greater scientific knowledge but to express a broader view of humanity than humans typically have of themselves. The space alien, coming from a great distance, is often depicted as being beyond the racial and nationalist identifications of humanity. It is no surprise then that when writers need to express a radical form of racial, cultural, and sexual inclusivity, they turn to this figure from beyond the stars. The space aliens discussed in this chapter can all be read as expressing views compatible with Gloria Anzaldúa's concept of the alien consciousness, her vision of a radically inclusive way of thinking and living, and each in its own unique way.[1]

Victuum (1976) by Isabella Rios (a pseudonym used by author Diana López) recounts the life of Valentina Ballesternos growing up in Oxnard, California, getting married, and having children. Valentina also has some extraordinary experiences involving an alien named Victuum. The novel is experimental in terms of narration. As Ramón Saldívar notes, "Victuum is a novel of pure dialogue"; Emily Maguire adds that some of this dialogue is interior dialogue (Saldívar 176; Maguire 353). This all-dialogue structure makes for an active read, as gaps in the plot must be filled in by the reader. In this novel, the space alien that Valentina encounters is not explicitly correlated with immigrants or Latinxs as a group; rather, Victuum is a teacher and becomes a source of enlightenment and self-acceptance for Valentina. The novel is divided into two different sections, with Victuum appearing in the second section.[2] The first section depicts the life of Valentina growing up in a Mexican American family. As Ritch Calvin writes: "Part One of Victuum reads, in some ways, like many of the early examples of Chicana/o literature. Ríos highlights the plight of women within Chicano culture and families; she represents the cultural biases against Chicanos in the West" (42). The second section takes a different turn as Valentina has a series of dream visions and psychic experiences in which she is visited by mythical and historical figures such as Medusa, William Wordsworth, and John F. Kennedy. The second section then has Valentina meeting Victuum, a space alien who is about four feet high, with "large almond shaped eyes," and who is from another "universe" (Rios 324–325). Victuum is a member of an alien race that is exploring the universe and he seems to have no intention of harming humanity but has come to study Earth (325). Ultimately, although the two sections of the novel are distinct, they are connected, and while only the second section is explicitly science fiction, it turns out that from the perspective of Victuum's science, the visions and ghosts from the first section are also science fiction.

The role that Victuum plays in the novel is primarily that of a teacher to Valentina. The section involving Victuum begins with Valentina's statement of ignorance: "I have so little knowledge. If only my brain would open to the mysteries of this universe, so that I may better understand" (324). Victuum then reveals these mysteries of the universe to her. Victuum, who communicates with Valentina through telepathy, also teaches her about the nature of the universe through a kind of virtual reality, multidimensional, photographic system (325). The scientific teaching he gives is based on the notion that sound units are the building blocks of the universe. In addition, before leaving her, Victuum shows Valentina a culturally and technologically advanced United States of the future. Valentina begins as ignorant of this advanced knowledge, and then over time gains the knowledge she seeks. At the same time, she was, according to Victuum, already more enlightened than many of the people who surround her, and this becomes clear in how Victuum affirms her antiracist views of the world.

As a teacher, Victuum is not just filling Valentina with facts; he is also something like a New Age teacher in that he attends to Valentina as more than a student and validates her experience in a number of ways. Valentina has some extraordinary capabilities that connect back to the beginning of the novel in which Valentina is described as being born with a "velo," a special birth covering, which indicated to the family that she would "know the spiritual world" (4). Victuum tells her, "Valentina you are irreplaceable" (325). She is also unique among humanity as a whole: "In actuality, people from my universe view mature human earthlings as children. Your planet is extremely young in comparison to ours. Though, you as an individual have the capacity to receive my mental telepathy" (325). Though some people in Valentina's community might deride Valentina's abilities, Victuum affirms that she is more highly evolved than other people.

The validation of Valentina's experience also comes through the language of science. Valentina has had some extraordinary experiences involving ghostly visits, powerful premonitions, and visions. These kinds of experiences are not typically acceptable in the society in which Valentina must interact. Valentina's mother, for example, often tells her to not let other people know about her experiences:

"I see him, Mama! . . ."
  "Who?"
  "A spirit . . . Mama . . . I see his spirit!"
  "Just don't tell anyone . . . no one . . . just tell me . . . people . . . they won't understand. . . . They will not understand . . . they'll call you crazy . . . they'll say you need to be put away. . . . So listen to me . . . don't tell anyone!" (152)

It turns out that these kinds of experiences are perfectly reasonable from the perspective of Victuum. Victuum's scientific explanations of these fantastic events have the effect in the novel of referring back to the previous sections. As for the visions of historical figures that Valentina has, Victuum explains, "They project their images as they envision themselves while they were in materialized state" (336–337). With regard to the telepathic communication between Victuum and Valentina, Valentina asks, "Victuum, your communication with me is transmitted through the process of extra sensory perception?" (337). Victuum responds: "Correct, Valentina, because thought is sound, and sound is also composed of energy, defined as magnetic force gravitation, which results in spiral circular formation of projection. All gravitation, as I have described before, has circular motion" (337). Through Victuum's explanation of the universe, such events are neither New Age nor superstition, but science, even if contemporary science is unaware of their truth. Astro traveling, extrasensory perception, and visitations from the past are all scientifically possible. Even more, the potential of the human mind is enormous: "The human brain has the capacity for universal control. With the use of thought energy force one may prevent death indefinitely. Death is the decomposition of tangible material. Primary sound does not decompose" (337). These claims may seem like spiritual fantasies, but they are real according to Victuum, and one day, the novel claims, science will catch up Victuum and Valentina.

This same sort of pattern of showing that Valentina is more enlightened than those around her is also seen in the passages that relate to race and ethnicity. Valentina's world is marked by poverty, racism, and sexism. She lives in a world that does not entirely accept her. She finds some solace in her family and barrio, but there are a number of aspects of her life that are rejected by society at large, in particular her race and her language. Although Valentina lives in something of a multiethnic environment, it is clear that Mexicans are subject to a great deal of racism, as in one instance, a boy in her class yells out: "'Ah teacher . . . when are those dirty Mexicans going to get out of our room and go back to their own school . . . or to their own room where they belong'" (67)? Nevertheless, Valentina is proud to be Mexican and stands up for herself and her family, calling the boy "mean" (67). Furthermore, Valentina is open-minded when it comes to race and nationality. She has positive relationships with people from multiple groups—Mexican, Anglo, Black—and is sympathetic to the Japanese who were interned during World War II. Victuum also affirms something that Valentina strongly believes, that her mother tongue, Spanish, is worthy of respect. Indeed, her family is proud to be Spanish speaking, and her father founded a Spanish-language newspaper. Nevertheless, Spanish was forbidden at school, as Valentina reports: "Everyone in class speaks Spanish . . . we all do . . . but no the teacher gets mad . . . she says we must speak American. . . . I don't know why . . . everyone understands Spanish" (11). Valentina is in fact punished for speaking Spanish, and yet Victuum is on her side and engages her in Spanish. According to Valentina: "He speaks to me in the language to which I am accustomed. He makes use of superb, exacting Spanish vocabulary" (324). The use of the space alien in the novel offers an imaginative space that demonstrates what it is like to radically embrace being Mexican and speaking Spanish, those elements of Valentina that have been rejected by Anglo society.

When Valentina is shown the future United States as part of Victuum's teaching, her inclusive perspective turns out to be justified. She observes one virtual image: "Is that the yellow race with calculating grey eyes I observe? They are flying with one-piece suits and transparent helmets." Victuum explains, "The yellow complexion is a result of the mating of Caucasian and Negroid races" (345). The simple detail is not meant to give a complete picture of future races but to show that these two groups that have historically been in conflict have come together. By seeing that different races can come together to create an advanced and enlightened culture, Valentina's own heritage as well as her views on race are shown to be enlightened and futuristic. Victuum teaches Valentina things that she could not possibly know otherwise; however, what she learns shows that the future will be more amenable to who she already is. Victuum brings enlightenment to Valentina, giving advanced knowledge and a higher perspective, and showing that a Chicanx woman is at the forefront of science as well as culture.

The context of *Victuum* provides some understanding as to how Rios is reclaiming a specific form of the space alien. Rios writes in the preface to the e-book edition, "Victuum is based on a true story of a young girl's odyssey in psychic discovery." She states that Valentina was a family member and that she interviewed her about her past and her experiences. With this information, *Victuum* is situated directly in the "contactee" biography tradition of space alien and UFO lore. Although there is no scientific evidence of the arrival of space aliens on planet Earth, they are scientifically possible, and the space alien does not merely function as a fictional character in U.S. culture. The space alien is a being that many people believe has engaged them, abducted them, or enlightened them. Victuum is certainly one of the enlightened space aliens, the "space brothers," which became popular in the 1950s. In particular, the novel shares key aspects of the work of George Adamski, who reported on his meeting with the space alien Orthon in his books *Flying Saucers Have Landed* and *Inside the Flying Saucers*. Adamski, like Rios, lived in Southern California, and he worked near the Palomar Observatory, which was the largest optical telescope for much of the twentieth century (Bader 76). In both Rios's and Adamski's books, the human and alien speak through telepathy, the alien is concerned about the atom bomb, the alien came in a small ship that had come out of a "mother ship," the alien has a supremely kind and giving personality. Even the names of the aliens, Orthon and Victuum, hearken back to Greek and Latin, giving the figures a kind of mysterious yet revered status.

The physical descriptions of Victuum and Orthon are very similar as well. Orthon and Victuum are smooth skinned, have almond Asiatic eyes and long fingers, and wear a one-piece spacesuit. Orthon, however, is also described as a type of alien called a "Nordic" or Aryan, and he has blond hair and gray-green eyes. Orthon is a "mixture of Nordic and 'Oriental'" features (Roth 52).[3] Adamski, in addition to being a contactee, was also a quasi-religious leader and was deeply influenced by Theosophy and its belief in aliens as a key to human evolution. His racial description of Orthon seems to come out of Theosophy's orientalism as well as its corresponding White supremacy. For Adamski, these blond, "Oriental" aliens were the paragon of beauty. Rios's Victuum, however, is only described as Asian-like, not Aryan or White. Most important, Victuum is not from Venus like Orthon but from "another universe" (Rios 325). In other words, Victuum has an even more distant perspective on humanity than Orthon. Victuum is more enlightened, more able to know the truth about the universe, and rather than speaking a sort of Asian language as Adamski describes it, Victuum speaks in Spanish. That Victuum validates Valentina's Mexican heritage and proud use of Spanish reclaims the enlightened space alien from its White supremacist space brother past.

While in *Victuum* the space alien is a repurposing of the Nordic aliens from the 1950s, in the short play *Bordertown* (2003) another sort of enlightened alien appears, though also connected to the UFO contactee tradition in California. First performed in 1998, the two-act play was written and performed by the performance comedy group Culture Clash.[4] The play is set in San Diego and features numerous characters from many racial or ethnic groups interacting and expressing their views about race and culture. UFOs appear a number of times in the play, in which they are either dropping aliens off or picking people up. A specific alien called the "bald man" appears once in the first act and then again in the final scene of the play (17). This character is wearing a "purple cosmic gown and Nike sneakers" (17), a reference to the clothing worn by the thirty-nine members of an actual UFO cult called Heaven's Gate who committed mass suicide in 1997 near the Palomar Observatory. Heaven's Gate was a cult that mixed religious beliefs with belief in space aliens, believing that if they were worthy enough through detachment from the physical world, their suicide would allow them to board a spaceship that was accompanying the Hale-Bopp Comet passing Earth (Rennie 144–147). That the outfit of the bald man in *Bordertown* is a reference to Heaven's Gate is confirmed when one character in the play expresses a fear that the reputation of the city would be tainted by the cult and their strange behavior. What Culture Clash did was to reclaim this figure for the Chicanx community in San Diego and turn its UFO cult beliefs into a powerful statement about race and culture.

The bald man addresses the audience directly and in the traditional space alien manner:

> Greetings, Earthlings. There are no borders in the cosmos, only infinitesimal [*sic*] possibilities. No one really dies; you just change frequency. The body disintegrates because it is made of atomic, earthly elements. However, our mind is a fourth-dimensional energy system. Transcending space and time, where there is no beginning or ending. We become in tune with the infinite. This is our higher self. (Culture Clash 17)

In addressing the audience as "Earthlings," he is highlighting the fact that he is a space alien, and as such, he would know firsthand about the nature of the cosmos. In this sense, these statements by the bald man are meant to teach the people, something like Victuum does with Valentina. However, the bald man is not offering a detailed scientific description of the nature of the universe; rather, the pronouncements are more in the style of a cult. The basic idea of the pronouncements is that humans have a higher self that is the spiritual or mental part of oneself that is separate from the body and will survive its disintegration. This is a pretty traditional view of enlightenment, that it is about the mind or spirit apart from the body. In assigning the mind as the higher self, the bald man is showing that the cosmic perspective, the higher view of life, is possible on Earth.

The bald man next takes on the role of a narrator in his speech by preparing the audience for what is about to take place in the play: "Therefore, prepare to escape from San Diego and leave behind your personal, cultural and political borders. Journey with us to the borderless cosmos, where race, creed, and religion does not matter" (Culture Clash 18). In the play, the audience will be taken outside of their normal life, their normal narrow view of the world, and will be presented with a variety of racial or ethnic groups of people. The play, and its daring crossing of many racial and ethnic borders, is then an exemplification of the higher view of life. By engaging in the play, the audience will in this sense be transported to the realm of the cosmos. What is interesting about this scenario is that the enlightenment that is offered is formed not through science but through art, in this case, drama. The audience members who are present at the actual performance of the play, or to a lesser degree the reader, engage in a kind of simulation of enlightenment by also looking down upon the depictions of race and creed. What the space alien prepares the audience for then happens, since many ethnic groups and perspectives on race are acted out throughout the play. There is a Chinese immigrant, a Pakistani American, a White middle-class couple, a White sheriff, a multiracial group of Navy guys, and so on. Many are immigrants or people who are outsiders, people who have experienced discrimination of one kind or another. Each of these groups is presented at least somewhat sympathetically, that is, their motivations, their mind (meaning their higher self) are shown. This is the case even when they are acting violently, as with the militiaman at the border who is given a chance to express his fears for his nation.

At the end of the play, the bald man returns again. This time he expresses a similar New Age philosophy as in his first speech but with some different imagery. He refers to the idea that humanity is at the end of "what the Aztecs call 'El Quinto Sol,'" a common image in the Chicanx movement. "El Quinto Sol" is the "dark age," a time of hatred and strife. In contrast, "the new millennium" will initiate a "spiritual renaissance of logic and reason" that will be guided by the higher self rather than the lower self (63). This is essentially the same message of enlightenment as in the beginning except it is put into a cosmic-historical context. The opening speech by the bald man is specifically about the audience, whereas the second speech puts it all into a larger social context. The use of the Aztec imagery connected to the future reclaims the speculative viewpoint of the Heaven's Gate philosophy. In addition, the bald man makes another interesting reference to Chicanx culture, "Our ancestors know of a place, a place where there are no borders, only infinitesimal [*sic*] possibilities" (63). The bald man's use of "our ancestors" is somewhat ambiguous, but it does seem to indicate that he is Chicanx and is emphasizing the Indigenous past. What does this mean, though, that the bald man is connected to being Chicanx?

How the bald man came to be a space alien can be explained by the abductions that happen to two other characters. In addition to the appearances of the bald man space alien, UFOs appear multiple times in the play. They appear before the two speeches by the bald man, presumably his mode of transportation. They also appear in the final scene of each act, right before two characters in the play are abducted by the aliens. These two characters, Chunky (Ramon Sanchez) and Queso (Salvador Roberto Torres), are depictions of actual community leaders in San Diego. Chunky is a musician and Queso is a muralist, and they were both involved in the development of Chicano Park and the Chicanx community in San Diego. Like the bald man's claim that the audience members can access their higher selves through the play itself, what is important about these two characters is that they are artists. In addition, their abduction can be interpreted as demonstrating that they are worthy, though not in the Heaven's Gate sense. If the bald man is connected to the Heaven's Gate cult, whose members wanted to be worthy and enlightened enough to be taken by the space aliens, then we can interpret these two characters as people who are worthy and important to the community and are enlightened people who can hold the aliens' views of racial and cultural harmony. This is a key reclamation of the Heaven's Gate philosophy, that what matters is community health rather than individual purity. In addition, this explains the possible origins of the bald man: that like Chunky and Queso he was taken up by the UFOs and has returned to Earth to tell humanity the truth of the cosmos.

It is also important that the inclusive philosophy of race and culture of the bald man is tethered by a strong Chicanx perspective specific to San Diego. This play, though expressing multiple racial and cultural perspectives, is centered on Chicanx history, and each of the two acts begins and ends with Chicanx characters historically framing the basic themes presented in the play. Furthermore, the first scenes of the two acts are set at the border. These scenes are mirror images of one another. The first act begins with two Chicanx actors in the United States who are mistaken for Mexican immigrants by the militiaman vigilante who stops them. The second act begins with the same two Chicanx actors in Mexico being mistaken for American drug runners who are caught by a character called "Mexican Militia Man" (39). In the first act, these characters are described as "MEXICAN 1 and 2" (10), whereas in the second they are "AMERICAN 1 and 2" (39). The idea is that Chicanxs are often seen by the gatekeepers as not belonging on either side of the border. Among Americans, they are called "wetbacks," and among Mexicans, they are *pochos*. At the same time, the final scenes of each act have a number of Chicanx characters discussing the history of the Chicanx community in San Diego, including the specific details of Chicano Park and the murals of the Coronado Bridge. These final scenes provide a counterpoint to the gatekeeping of the opening scenes, in that they show a space made for the unique cultural mixing of Chicanxs in the United States. In addition, in both acts, though the two characters are not in fact immigrants, they are identified with immigrants. The play ends with characters forming the silhouette of the iconic border crossing sign of a man, woman, and child crossing the border, giving a final image of Chicanxs united with immigrants in solidarity. This ambivalent cultural mixing of Mexican and American that is indicative of *Bordertown*, combined with a strong empathy and identification with immigrants, is a hallmark of Chicanx thinking and it gives the play its foundation.

There are a number of other characters in the play who also express a similar enlightened view of racial inclusivity as the bald man. Two of the most overt are a White ex-marine cowboy-like figure who lives in Mexico, and a hippie Chicanx named Cosmico, both of whom express a strong antiracist philosophy. Both are also people who have explicitly crossed cultural borders, as Cosmico connects to White hippie culture and the ex-marine connects to Mexican border culture. Each of them enacts their antiracism in their family lives to a certain extent, as both married outside of their own ethnic group. They are living the philosophies that they espouse. At the end of the first act, Cosmico reads a science fiction poem that expresses his view:

> Flying saucers in the air
> fly high like the huelga eagle
> above the Coronado
> soaring high high
> above Aztlan lan lan lan, lan lan lan
> recuerdos de mi pueblo
> mi San Diego that I love
> a San Diego for all gentes, all peoples
> brown, black, yellow, red and, yes, even white. (36)

In this case, the connection is made between the visual perspective that the UFO has and the ethical perspective. The UFO is high above and sees all from a distance. The UFO sees San Diego as a whole, not a San Diego divided into racial groups. The "huelga eagle" here most likely refers to the eagle on the flag of the UFW (United Farm Workers) union. Curtis Marez observes a similar image with regard to the flag of the NFLU (National Farm Labor Union), with its "image of an eagle hovering over the earth," which represents the "planetary perspective" of the union that is "race- and gender-integrated" (*Farm Worker Futurism* 51). In other words, the goal of this farm workers union was to unite different groups to maintain a stronger stance against agribusiness. The poem also expresses the identity of Cosmico. In the line "recuerdos de mi pueblo," it is suggested that a traditional Mexican village will be the reference, but this is upended by referring to San Diego, a bustling city in the United States. Neither the view of the UFOs nor the memories of Cosmico are nationalistic; they are a vision of a multiethnic collective. Cosmico, as well as the ex-marine, in a certain sense, are already living the "space alien" lifestyle.

The perspective offered by the bald man can be critiqued on one level as unrealistic or utopian, in the sense of trying to downplay or ignore racial conflict. It is certainly possible that this aspect of the play is interpreted by some viewers as utopian. There is much in the play that works against this critique, however. First, the content of many of the stories told by the various characters is not one of different races coming together happily. Most often, the stories involve violence and hatred, and ignorance of one another. Incidents such as the Zoot Suit Riots are mentioned as forming part of the social landscape, for example. In addition, the racism of various groups is often satirized. This is not an idealized view of these different groups of people and how they relate. The enlightened vision of San Diego is itself also made fun of by the characters themselves and it is correlated with a kind of hippie pot-smoking viewpoint. As one character says twice with regard to the UFOs as well as all the strange views of the people: "This place is fucking weird" (Culture Clash 17, 63). Nevertheless, even as the play avoids many of the pitfalls of the idealized viewpoint that claims to be beyond race, it does still demonstrate to a certain degree the power of this idea of radical inclusivity.

While *Bordertown* and *Victuum* depict space aliens who act essentially as a teacher of a radically inclusive society, Ernest Hogan's novel *Cortez on Jupiter* (1990) gives a more direct representation of the alien consciousness. The novel is in fact focused on the nature of the protagonist's consciousness, and as Anzaldúa describes it, the alien consciousness is often "an inner war" (*Borderlands/La Frontera* 100). The novel is centered on Pablo Cortez and his artistic exploits across the solar system. It begins on Earth, or the "Mudball" as it is called in the novel (69), as Cortez joins up with a group of art school students to form the Guerilla Muralistas of Los Angeles. After a particularly high-profile artwork project involving the group painting the freeway, the group is arrested and forced to do community service. Cortez opts to join the Space Culture Project (SCP) and is then sent off to space to work in Hightown, an off-Earth city, where he begins his work doing splatter painting, a variation of Jackson Pollock's "drip" method but in low gravity. While at Hightown, Cortez volunteers for a particularly dangerous mission at the Ithaca space station above Jupiter. There he interacts with a powerful alien entity, a consciousness that surrounds the planet of Jupiter. Unlike his predecessors, Cortez survives the contact, but he is never the same afterward.

The space aliens in this story, called the Sirens, are not like the individual alien figures of *Victuum* and *Bordertown*. The sirens are described this way: "These single-celled creatures interact with electrical activity that theorists compare to brain activity—for which the term 'zapware' was coined" (Hogan, *Cortez* 22). In other words, the alien is something like an enormous brain that covers the planet. It is essentially the atmosphere of Jupiter and its communication center is the Big Red Spot. Humanity does not fully understand the Sirens, and yet undertakes the mission to send people into the atmosphere of Jupiter to try to communicate. In every instance prior to Cortez, however, the Sirenauts (astronauts who meet the Sirens) die as a result of the encounter. Cortez describes what happens to the people: "It's the mind getting yanked out of the brain, into the Siren's Big Red Synaptic Center . . . the Sirenaut always goes soft, opens up, lets go, and is gone, gone, gone" (161). Cortez, however, survives the interaction. The problem with the previous Sirenauts was that they were either too rigid in their way of thinking or too open and contemplative, letting everything come inside without filters. Cortez tries to create a balance, which he enacts through his imagination. He says, "Because my imagination is powerfulísimo enough to face what most people find unthinkable" (179). In addition to his ability to take in the images produced by the alien, he is not overwhelmed by them, a feat performed by imagining painting them, "The images would go from incoherent to incomprehensible to bizarre to familiar as I struggled to paint them in my cabeza" (192). Cortez is able to take the enormous amount of images coming into him, filter them, and then manipulate them into art. In this case, it is imaginary art that saves him, and it is art that serves to enable enlightenment rather than death. Later, when Cortez is back at the space station and out of the coma that he endures as a result of the experience, he is now able to paint in reality, not just in his head. The Sirens remain in his head, and so he has an endless flow of images that come to him. This ability to take in what others cannot and then make something new out of it is a powerful foundation for an alien consciousness that is radically inclusive.

Cortez's way of thinking and ability to withstand multiplicity mirrors his views on his racial and cultural background. His views on his own race are above anything else restless and at times unbearable. At various times in the novel, he identifies with or says he is connected to being Chicano, Aztec, Spanish, Mexican, Anglo, African, and alien. At the same time, this means that he is not entirely identified with any of these categories. Possibly most fundamental is that he is a Chicano, or Mexican American, and is pretty classically so. He speaks in Spanglish and says, "I was raised neo-Aztec in a relocated barrioid" (43). In describing his parents, he says that they are "college-educated Chicano intellectuals" (13). Cortez sees himself as a Chicano. It should be noted, however, that being Chicano is itself a category that is centered on the mixing of races and cultures, as described in the pivotal Chicano poem "Yo Soy Joaquin," in which the narrator identifies as Spanish, Indigenous, Mexican, and finally, Mexican American.

In addition to the focus on the cultural mixing of Chicanos, the Indigenous elements of Cortez make up quite a bit of the novel as well, and are consistent with the Chicano revival of Aztec mythology. Cortez mentions his parents who taught him Nahuatl (47), and one character describes him as looking similar to an Aztec warrior and having a "classic Aztec nose and cheekbones" (18). Much of the novel is Cortez describing what he is doing in terms of Aztec gods and goddesses; for example, the brothers Quetzalcoatl and Tezcatlipoca embody the spirit and the body for Cortez, and he uses these figures to explain his view that both spirit and body are important (240). At times, in distinction to the Spanish, he strongly identifies with the Indigenous. He says that the Aztec gods "were *mine*, not property of the light-skinned aliens from 'back-east'—they were *my* heritage, it was *my* blood that stained those pyramids, *my* art that survived the campaign of another Cortés centuries ago" (180; emphasis in original). In this case, even though he matches his name with the colonizing Spanish, he distances himself from them through a powerful self-identification with the Aztecs. Obviously, though, this connection to Aztec culture is gleaned through history more than contemporary Indigenous groups and he realizes that he is not fully Indigenous. He says: "Somebody actually called me white once. In Mexico. An Indio" (156). In other words, he realizes that even though in the United States he would not likely be identified as White, to an Indigenous person he is more European than Indigenous. In the last chapter, he calls the Aztec part of him "this otherness," indicating that it is a piece of him rather than his only identity (237).

At the same time, even though he does distance himself from the Spanish he also identifies himself a number of times in the novel with Cortez as a conqueror. Near the end of the novel, when Cortez is something of a hero for surviving the meeting with the Sirens, he says: "I am Cortés Nuevo! Conqueror of the Solar System!" (229). Ironically, he also couches the first contact with the aliens as a colonial moment in which the Sirens are more like Cortés, whereas the humans, himself included, are more like the Aztecs. Humans are, after all, dying from meeting the Sirens. This basic and ongoing tension among Chicano, Mexican, Aztec, and Spanish is the primary tension of the character. He says: "I came together like some Frankenstein monster out of bits of Spanish conquistador centaurs and Aztec Indian warriors. . . . So what am I, Spanish or Mexican?" (197). The idea is that there are all of these parts, but they are not coherently put together into some harmony, as Anzaldúa notes as important to the alien consciousness, and he has a sense that he belongs nowhere, which makes him a unique synthesis. He is the child of war, Spanish and Indigenous in conflict. Cortez is an alien consciousness in the making, and yet as Anzaldúa notes, it is an "inner war."

There are a number of other alien elements that are added to Cortez's alien consciousness. First is the fact that even after Cortez is pulled out of the atmosphere of Jupiter, he is still connected to the Sirens. It seems that the Sirens are there to stay, in his mind at least. He clearly expresses the difficulties of the alien consciousness, and yet he revels in it as it gives him a constant source of images for his art. He has received a form of cosmic enlightenment, knowing things about the universe that no one else knows, and yet it is painful. From this alien consciousness he receives all sorts of information, diagrams of advanced technology, images of faraway planets, and so on. Cortez was the first to engage the Sirens and survive, but then he takes the alien back to human society, not as an invasion, but as the potential for the enlightenment of humanity. In addition, Cortez has an intimate experience with his co-worker and lover, Willa Semba, a powerful empath from South Africa, and as a result she also enters into his mind. Not only through their sexual encounter but also after his contact with the Sirens, she enters his mind along with her African culture. This makes for a wild and confusing mental state for Cortez: "Signals get all log-jammed. The paint calls. The Sirens call. Willa calls—" (239). She in fact becomes his muse: "Ay, qué Willa! In all the jumble of visions, paint, zapware, and Sirens, you are always with me. I feel you constantly. You are alive" (243). In this way, Cortez is a protomember of *la raza cósmica*, with a radically inclusive alien consciousness in the making. Finally, Cortez's consciousness and his way of thinking are at the center of the novel's structure. It is his unique consciousness that is accepting of cultural ambiguity, which allows him to interact and survive the meeting with the Sirens. The novel's form is a representation of this consciousness. The first and final sections of the novel are directly narrated by Cortez. The chapters in between, however, are a depiction of a television interview with Cortez as done by television personality Anna Paik. In this middle part of the novel, other characters are interviewed, reports are shown, there is dramatic dialogue, and multiple points of view are expressed. The multiplicity of the novel is not just postmodern pastiche but a manifestation of the challenges of living with the alien consciousness.

The space alien, as an enlightened being, has often expressed a similar philosophy as Anzaldúa's alien consciousness, that humans have the potential to attain a radically inclusive way of being. In the stories discussed in this chapter, there are various ways that the alien consciousness is formed. In *Victuum*, the alien consciousness of Valentina is just beginning since the space alien plays the role of a teacher who validates the experiences of Valentina using the language of a futuristic science. In *Bordertown*, it is the city, San Diego, that forms the outline of the alien consciousness. Within that outline, all races and ethnicities can be included. For the viewer or reader, however, it is art that provides this broad vision. In *Cortez on Jupiter*, the alien consciousness is given a more direct representation, since the story is focused on the consciousness of

Cortez, who then takes the next step toward joining with an actual space alien. In this case, art is not just a means to gaining a broader perspective; it is a means of survival, to manage the confusing borderlands experience. Humans have often projected the best of humanity onto the fictional space alien, as is the case with these three narratives. As an expression of the alien consciousness, the space alien becomes a means to imagine a better world than our actual world filled with systematic and pervasive racism and oppression of the poor. As one character from the novel *Lunar Braceros 2125–2148* writes:

> When we were kids, space was, for us, the unknown, the universe, full of stars and planets and comets, an infinite area of exploration that would undoubtably bring us into contact with beings of higher intelligence, more highly evolved, that would revolutionize our world and change social relations and put an end not only to our ignorance about so many things, but also, to especially, to the reservations. (12)

The enlightened space alien is, in a sense, the most positive and utopian-leaning figure in science fiction, and as such, it is a key part of forming the alien consciousness. In this way, the figure of the space alien is a measure of the hope in humanity. Just as we can project the best of humanity onto the space alien, however, we can also project our worst, most violent selves. The next chapter takes on this completely different sort of space alien, the one that arrives as a source of horror.

6

Space Aliens and the
Discovery of Horror

■ ■ ■ ■ ■ ■ ■ ■ ■ ■ ■ ■ ■ ■ ■ ■ ■ ■ ■ ■

This chapter is in many ways the black mirror image of the preceding chapter. Whereas the space aliens in the last chapter expressed the radical inclusivity of Anzaldúa's alien consciousness, the space aliens here express the limits of the alien consciousness, the all-to-human inability to embrace all that is alien. Space aliens who come from a distance with their advanced science and technology can reasonably be assumed to have a broader view of humanity, a view that we are simply not capable of, and so they are often depicted as being enlightened. Alternatively, this distant perspective on humanity and advanced science and technology can also result in space aliens feeling that they are completely superior to humans, or being unconcerned about the fate of humanity, or even acting in malicious and hostile ways toward humanity.

The short stories discussed in this chapter contain a key element of horror connected to the space alien, a part in which a character or reader discovers a horrifying yet liberating truth that begins to move in the direction of the alien consciousness. One common framework for understanding the horror genre is that it demonstrates a "return of the repressed," that is, some aspect of society that has been repressed and that can be expressed in the violent atmosphere of horror (Wood 69). This framework, however, like that of the "Other," is too engaged with the White gaze in the sense that it focuses on how horror indulges in a temporary release of the racial or sexual Others. This chapter is formed with a different framework based on the idea that the discovery of horror is at once terrifying and liberating. Like any migrant, the space alien upsets the status quo, and this can be a horrifying experience for those who are settled in their routine. Vilém Flusser in his philosophy of migration describes the general status quo of a society: "Custom and habit are a blanket that covers over reality as it exists" (81). In our comfort zone as it were, we cannot see reality for what it is, for it is covered by habit. The migrant, however, often experiences life with the blanket of habit torn away, living a life of discovery and uncovered reality. This may be a source of terror:

> Discovery begins as soon as the blanket is pulled away. Everything is then seen as unusual, monstrous, and "unsettling" in the true sense of the word. To understand this one merely has to consider one's own right hand and finger movements from the point of view of, say, a Martian. It becomes an octopus-like monstrosity. (82)

The Martian sees the hand as an appendage, similar to one of its own tentacles, and yet it is shaped differently and has strange hard tips (nails). The migrant passes this new sort of perspective into society, unsettling the status quo, creating horror, but at the same time, the uncovered is a liberation from habit. That the space alien has the capability to understand herself, her society, her world from an alien perspective is one of the most important, and at times frightening, values of the space alien.

These horrific stories are very much the cousin of the detective fiction genre, which also relies on this mode of discovery. The method whereby the horror is discovered is typically different than the detective story, however, because the protagonists do not want to uncover the occluded horror, or at least regret it when they do, and unlike the detective genre, the status quo in these horrific stories is not returned at the end of the story; in fact, the end is typically where the horror begins. The mode of discovery is significant because it guides how the horrific space aliens are integrated into the plot. The tension of the story is created by the lead-up to the discovery, the clues and hints that something is amiss. At times, the discovery happens to a character, such as when a monster jumps out of the closet, while at other times, the characters are not even aware of the horror, a situation that is in many ways even more horrifying. In the first two stories, Pablo Brescia's "Code 51" and Junot Díaz's "Monstro," there is a depiction of the protagonists discovering the horror of alien take-over, even if they are resistant to its arrival, but in the next two stories, Daína Chaviano's "The Annunciation" and Mercurio Rivera's "Dance of the Kawkawroons," the protagonists do not completely experience the horror because they do not come to full awareness of the horrible events taking place. The protagonists may feel the fear, and deeply at times, but they have no real knowledge of what is happening—these horrors are for the reader to discover.

Pablo Brescia's short story "Code 51," included in *Latinx Rising: An Anthology of Latinx Science Fiction and Fantasy* (2020), begins one evening as Steve Torres receives a phone call reporting a flying saucer near the home of the woman he loves, Susan Navajo. Torres, the sheriff of Chupadero, New Mexico (population 351), heads to the house along with Sergeant Wilson, who is obsessed with films about space aliens. At the house, the plot turns, and Wilson indicates that he is going to kill Torres, and that the phone call was an elaborate hoax he created with Grandma Navajo and Susan. This turns out to be untrue, as becomes clear when Grandma Navajo kills Wilson and then makes a proclamation about the arrival of space aliens: "We have waited many cycles. The time for unification has arrived. Susan Navajo and Steve Torres, you who came from another time and place, are twin halves. You are our salvation. This land is diseased and must be purified. They, our own, have returned. The children of the gods have come back to take what is rightfully theirs" (14). A spaceship appears, shooting out some kind of liquid, and as Susan and Steve swim through the liquid, they are surprisingly able to breath. When Torres realizes that they have gills, and therefore that they are some kind of space alien, he reacts: "Susan, his dear Susan, swam back to him. When their bodies touched, he noticed the gills. And in the face of sheriff Steve Torres horror set in" (15). The horror from seeing their gills is a moment of body horror, a revulsion to the fish-like gills. In addition, the gills are also a sign that they are now space aliens. Since human identity is so deeply tied to distinguishing itself from other species, terrestrial or extraterrestrial, to cross that boundary is to separate oneself, even if in some small way, from the rest of humanity. In that sense, to give a character gills, is a way to move in the direction of separating the characters from humanity, alienizing them. The horrific body transformation here causes revulsion, and it causes terror at the loss of human identity.

Every reaction of horror has a context. In this case, the fact that Torres is a space alien was covered over and hidden in his previous life. The moment of horror, then, can be expressed as him realizing that who he thought he was is not who he actually is. This context of the moment of horror is intertwined with the characterization of Torres, since prior to the discovery, he is portrayed as being alienated from himself and his environment. He is constantly annoyed by his sergeant, and by having to live in such a small town with people who are reporting UFOs all the time. As part of his alienation, he adopts a professional persona and is insistent on fulfilling his duty, both of which help in distancing him from his feelings about his work and his town. When he takes the call about the Navajos at the beginning of the story, the narrator states that he "seems concerned," indicating that his insistence on duty is to a degree faked. In addition, the police station is described using this ironic phrase: "The police station was a clean, well-lighted place. Everything there served the truth" (11).[1]

It is clear, however, that the police station did not serve the truth, since Torres after all did not even believe in UFOs or space aliens prior to his awareness of the truth. This dedication to his perfunctory professional duty is mirrored by his lack of expression of personal passion. He is in love with Susan Navajo, yet does not act on it, a fact he is aware of: "*Five years have gone by, what am I waiting for?*, he asked himself" (13; italics in original). Torres's alienation is also expressed by his only hobby, which is reading about "ancient civilizations," as well as his asthma, which indicates that he is not physically comfortable with Earth's environment (13). Torres's alienation from his true self is strong, as the narrator reports, "He thought he was going to die and that it didn't matter because he had been dead for many years" (15). Before he realizes that he is an alien, Torres is alienated. The consequence of this state of being is that Torres is not prepared to accept the truth. In this way, part of the horror experienced by Torres is its immediacy, the shock of suddenly having the covering of habit lifted from his life, and seeing himself as he actually is.

Torres's horror is intertwined with a liberation from these barriers to him seeing the truth. This is directly expressed by the immediate curing of his asthma, apparent after being engulfed by the alien water: "Torres felt something in his gut. Now under water, he breathed better. He was no longer afraid" (15). Significantly, Torres and Susan touch for what is presumably the first time, breaking down the walls that kept them apart. Torres seems aware of this change after hearing the proclamation of Grandma Navajo: "Torres felt he was inside an absurd nightmare from which he did not want to wake. The woman was obviously crazy, but her madness might also mean his liberation" (15). It is important to note that this liberation is not an ultimate liberation, as the story ends: "The truth, finally, was beginning to make way" (15). What a complete liberation for Torres would look like, readers will most likely never know. This moment of easement and feeling of potential liberation is short lived, but it promises a more authentic life once the horror of his new alien life is embraced.

The personal liberation is also tied to a larger social liberation that is part of an allegorical reading of the story, as signaled by Susan Navajo's last name. If she is the Native personified, then Wilson is the Anglo, and Torres is the Latinx. The situation of the border, as Anzaldúa writes, is as such: "Gringos in the U.S. Southwest consider the inhabitants of the borderlands transgressors, aliens— whether they possess documents or not, whether they're Chicanos, Indians or Blacks" (*Borderlands/La Frontera* 25). This truth, that Anglos think that people of color are aliens in the Southwest, is covered over by Anglos. Wilson, however, at the moment he is revealing his purported alliance with the Navajos, reveals his racism. Wilson yells at Torres as he holds Susan: "At the end of the day, you're a fuckin' Mexican living on our land. You don't belong here, understand? As far as I'm concerned Chupadero can be sucked into the desert! You're about to die and we're leaving. Susan, say goodbye to your boyfriend"

(Brescia 14). Wilson believes he is a space alien, but it seems he is wrong, and it is Torres and the Navahos who are the actual space aliens. It is the space aliens who are the actual Natives, however, and Wilson is the actual alien in the Southwest. The uncovering of the horrible truth of Wilson's racism is also the moment of liberation as well since the allegorical reading points to the truth of the racial relations that is covered over by Anglos, and of course the historical reality is that the Whites are the aliens to the Southwest. The Mexican and Native Americans are then the ones who will take part in the new water world as Anglo colonization of the American Southwest ends.

Beyond the personal horrors of Torres and the social horrors of racism, the language of the story itself expresses a liberating horror concerning the more general matter of truth and fiction. This aspect is present in the myriad uses of the language of art, theater, and film in the story. One characteristic of Wilson, for example, that expresses his relationship to truth is his obsession with film. He says after the initial phone call from the Navahos: "'Boss, don't you think this would be a good scene from one of those detective movies from the 1940s? Picture it: It's midnight, somebody calls, we go a mystery! We're smoking of course, and you say: 'We'll be by shortly.' Don't you think?'" (12). Wilson repeats this correlation of their experience with a scene from a movie twice more, once in reference to *Close Encounters of the Third Kind* (1977) and then in reference to *Alien* (1979). As Wilson ironically states: "'You are an idiot, sheriff, you really are. Haven't you seen *Alien*? The enemy is *inside*'" (14; italics in the original). Although Wilson is using the correct film reference, he is wrong in how it relates to the world, that is, it is Torres who is the space alien, whereas Wilson is just a human.

In addition, it seems that all the characters in the story are being moved by forces beyond them and not by their own authentic decisions. When Wilson grabs Susan and is about to kill Torres, he makes a "move that looked choreographed" (14). This language is also used with regard to Grandma Navajo, as her speech to Torres and Susan is described as "seemingly reciting a script" (14). Finally, truth is also mediated for the reader as well, as expressed by the metafictional element of the story, instances of which are scattered throughout. The story begins:

> A light flashed across the horizon.
>   Suddenly, the phone rang. *The telephone always rings "suddenly,"* he thought.
> (11; italics in the original)

The narrator uses the term "suddenly" to describe the phone ringing, and then the character thinks about the same phone ring using the same term. This strange and comedic connection is made between the narrator and the character in a situation in which they are pretty clearly not the same entity. This connection therefore brings to the surface the scripted nature of the story, that a writer can connect a character and a narrator even if they are not the same person. The wall separating the story from the reader is broken down as well since the reader mysteriously connects to Torres's thoughts. When a reader is reading a story there must be some sense of a suspension of disbelief, that is, a provisional belief in the truth of that fictional world. A metafictional element puts that belief in the truth of the story in question. This is the uncovering of a horrible truth, that there is no truth behind the fiction. "Code 51" points to the script, the overarching presence that appears like the return of a horrible yet liberating space alien. The horrible knowledge that the protagonist discovers at the end of the story is that he is himself a space alien, separated from humanity. The reader finds herself in the same position, separated forever from the truth of the story, yet now free from the border that fiction raises between itself and readers.

Junot Díaz's "Monstro," an excerpt from a potential novel and included in *Latinx Rising: An Anthology of Latinx Science Fiction and Fantasy* (2020), is narrated by an unnamed Dominican student from Brown University who visits the Dominican Republic for the summer. The narrator, an aspiring novelist, meets up with Alex, a rich friend from Brown, and Mysty, a woman with whom he falls hopelessly in love. The three of them take advantage of their vacation time and Alex's wealth to hang out, take photographs, and go on excursions. The story takes place in the near future at a time of economic troubles and ecological degradation, with the rich living in domes while the rest suffer in the extreme heat. In this dystopian yet plausible future, things get worse, in the form of what seems to be an extraterrestrial virus that begins to infect the most vulnerable and sick people in Haiti. The victims then experience a radical transformation. They go through a period of "Silence," then they begin a coordinated screaming/singing activity called the "Chorus," then they become murderous, and finally they grow into "Forty-Foot-tall cannibal motherfuckers running loose on the island" (101). The United States, which had mostly ignored the problems in Haiti, finally reacts and demolishes Port-au-Prince with bombs. The story ends with the narrator and his friends heading toward the Haitian border to try to witness firsthand what is going on there. In this part of the story, the narrator does not directly experience the alien horrors. It is implied that he will later confront the aliens directly, but in this part of the story, all alien horrors are indirect and mediated.

"Monstro" is set in the near future, but there are three separate time periods to keep in mind. The earliest period involves the beginning of the outbreak of the virus when the narrator is hanging out with Alex and Mysty. This comprises the primary plot of this part of the novel. The middle period begins with the bombing of Port-au-Prince and involves the narrator confronting the monsters in Haiti. This middle period is the future, from the perspective of the first part of the story. The last period is the present time of the narrator, as he tells the story about his involvement in the tragedy, after having discovered the horrible truths of the world. It is not clear how far in the future it is, but he does have a somewhat wry perspective on his younger self. The middle period is when the narrator experiences direct alien horrors. It is in this period that the three protagonists head into Haiti and witness the giants. This is clear because the narrator mentions a photograph of the giants taken during the middle period. Although there is no direct mention, it is implied that Alex is the photographer who took the Polaroid "showing what later came to be called a Class 2 in the process of putting a slender broken girl in its mouth" (101). They experienced this horror, and presumably many others during this period, and yet, in the first time period, this confrontation is discussed as the future of the younger narrator. During that time, their experience is mediated through technology (photography) and through writing: "Beneath the photo someone had scrawled: Numbers 11:18. *Who shall give us flesh to eat?*" (101). Though not stated directly, it can be assumed that the "someone" is the narrator putting horror to poetry.

Before the narrator and his two friends experience the horrors of the alien invasion, it is the Haitians who are primarily affected, but these horrors are always mediated for the young narrator in the early period of the story. What happens to the Haitian victims of the virus is only seen through the near-future digital technology, and the terms used are new: "Whorl" seems like a future internet, and the "glypts" seems like a form of image-text communication (81–82). The first case of the virus was a four-year-old boy: "By the time his uncle brought him in his arm looked like an enormous black pustule, so huge it had turned the boy into an appendage of the arm. In the glypts he looked terrified" (81). Other depictions are less focused on the horror of the Haitians and more focused on the reactions of disgust at the horrors. The narrator describes how the virus begins to work on the body: "The black mold-fungus-blast that came on a splotch and then gradually started taking you over, tunneling right through you" (81). The virus seems at first like an aggressive kind of mold that takes over the body, but over time, the people infected begin to fuse:

> I remember the first time I saw it on the Whorl. Alex was, like Mira esta vaina. Almost delighted. A shaky glypt of a pair of naked trembling Haitian brothers sharing a single stained cot, knotted together by horrible mold, their heads slurred into one. About the nastiest thing you ever saw. Mysty saw it and looked away and eventually I did, too. (82)

The central focus of this quote is not so much the brothers, but the three differing reactions to the image. This mediation of digital technology does connect the protagonists to the horrors of the Haitians, but at the same time separates them. This separation, ultimately, makes it possible to just look away, or as with the case of Alex, to gaze upon the horrors with a degree of pleasure.

The protagonists' disgust at the horrors the Haitians are experiencing is mirrored by the narrator's reaction to his mother's sickness. The appearance of his mother, who was the reason that the narrator came to the Dominican Republic in the first place, makes him uncomfortable and he describes her looking "like a stick version of herself" (83). His reaction is not only disgust but a desire to leave, to look away. He describes the sickness this way: "The year before, she'd been bitten by a rupture virus that tore through half her organs before the doctors got savvy to it" (83). The narrator's description of his mother's virus and the alien virus are strangely similar, connecting the narrator's resistance to these two horrible truths. Although he is sympathetic to the victims in both cases, the barriers to confronting these truths remain intact. Self-conscious about this lack of sympathy for his mother at the time, he addresses the reader from his future position: "What an asshole, right? What a shallow motherfucker. But I was nineteen—and what is nineteen, if not for shallow" (83)? Ultimately, the resistance to his mother's plight is consistent with his resistance to the plight of the Haitians, and it is made possible by his economic status.

It is not simply their personal resistance that separates the protagonists from the horrors. The horrors are continually mediated in a variety of ways related to their characters and their economic status. This is expressed by the general economic situation of the three friends that allows them to enjoy their summer in the relative safety of Alex's domed apartment. The three friends are buffered from the effects of climate change and the despair, and they go outside only when they want an adventure. In addition, both Alex and the narrator are artist types who are constantly seeing the world through a fictional lens. The primary mediating effect of "Monstro," however, is found in its being structured with a foreground and a background, alternating between the narrator explaining the details of the virus's effects and what the three friends are doing to pass the time on the island. In an interview, Díaz describes the two levels of narration and the two genres working in the story:

> I just loved the idea of these over-privileged doofuses pursuing what we would call a "mainstream" or "literary fiction" narrative, while in the background, just out of their range—though they could see it if they wished to see it—there's a much more extreme, horrifying narrative unfolding. ("Junot Díaz Aims")

The literary fiction part is describing the three friends while the science fiction aspect describes the virus. In other words, the three characters party while the world falls apart. The two narrative streams, and genres, begin to come together at the end of the story, when the three friends are entering Haiti and are about to confront the horror on the island.

The horrors for the three friends themselves truly begin at the end of "Monstro," with the bombing of Port-au-Prince by the U.S. military (100). In addition to the thousands killed, one of the effects of this bombing is an electromagnetic pulse that kills all electronic devices within a six-hundred-mile radius. The origin of the pulse is not clearly stated, but it seems most likely that it was the aliens who created the pulse. The loss of electricity causes a loss of internet, as well as the ability to maintain the domes that keep wealthy communities safe from the environment. This loss is the moment when the narrator and his friends finally begin to be affected by the alien horrors. Alex's domed apartment no longer keeps out the heat, and they see the horrors surrounding them, the fires spreading, and the "craziness" in the streets (101). Although these are not direct experiences with the aliens, the truth was making its way out at this point. The uselessness of most technologies means that the mediation is no longer possible. It is their liberation from that particular wall. The literal walls that surround them are destroyed as well, since their dome will no longer protect them from the violence on the street. If the problem is that the narrator and his friends are separated from the truth, then the horror is a liberation, a breaking down of the walls that are raised by their class loyalty.

What Díaz is highlighting through the dual narrative of "Monstro" is the common response of ignoring or suppressing horror. However, as he expresses in his nonfiction essay on Haiti "Apocalypse: What Disasters Reveal," it is precisely such horrors that can lay bare important injustices of the world. Díaz writes: "After all, if these types of apocalyptic catastrophes have any value it is that in the process of causing things to fall apart they also give us a chance to see the aspects of our world that we as a society seek to run from, that we hide behind veils of denials." In other words, the horrors are already there in Haiti, but people ignore them. It is a difficult task, of course, to face these disasters, and to face the truths that they reveal, but as Díaz argues, "Haiti is also a sign of what is to come." The fate of Haiti is the fate of the world. This means that by looking to Haiti, a way forward may be found, as Haiti has done before with its society built from a slave revolt. What does this future of the world look like? Díaz describes it: "What we will be left with will be a stricken, forlorn desolation, a future out of a sci-fi fever dream where the super-rich will live in walled-up plantations of impossible privilege and the rest of us will wallow in unimaginable extremity, staggering around the waste and being picked off by the hundreds of thousands by 'natural disasters'—by 'acts of god.'" To face the disasters of the Caribbean is not a minor act, and it can be the first step in saving the world from a global apocalypse. Horror is the first step of a potential liberation for the planet.

In the next two stories, the protagonists do not gain a full awareness of the horror, but they experience what readers believe to be horrible events. That is to say, if the protagonists were fully aware of what was happening, they would be horrified. Daína Chaviano's short story "The Annunciation" from *Cosmos Latinos: An Anthology of Science Fiction from Latin America and Spain* (2003) rewrites the annunciation story contained in the Christian Bible and transforms it into science fiction. The story can best be described as a secret history in which Jesus was actually a space alien, thereby explaining why he could perform miracles and rise from the dead. In the original version of the annunciation in the Gospel of Luke, the angel Gabriel comes to Mary to tell her that she will have a child and name him Jesus. The child will be conceived through divine intervention: "The Holy Spirit will come on you, and the power of the Most High will overshadow you" ("The Birth of Jesus Foretold"; Luke 1:26–38). Although Mary is frightened, she accepts her fate. Chaviano's story retains key aspects of this original story; however, it diverges sharply by depicting Gabriel not as an angel of God but as a space alien. His leader, Iab-eh, and the other aliens, it seems, have been interacting with humans for a while. Most important, Gabriel comes not only to announce the conception of Jesus but to enact it as well, and over the course of the story, Gabriel seduces Mary, they have sex, and Jesus is conceived.

The character of Mary does not explicitly experience horror in the story; instead, she experiences great fear. Throughout the entire encounter, Mary is shown to be experiencing fear through a variety of descriptors: "troubled," "upset," "disturbed," "alarmed," "anguish," and "invaded by some vague and unknown fear" (Chaviano, "Annunciation" 203, 204, 205, 205, 205, 206). This fear arises from the fact that an angel of God is in her home, that her husband is not there, and most important, that she has no experience with sex and is being seduced. From the perspective of the reader, however, who also sees the overall behavior of Gabriel, as well as the space aliens' actions in general, there is more happening in the story. The horror in the story is not experienced by Mary but is created by the situation of dramatic irony, which is a reading scenario in which the reader knows or understands something that a character in the story does not. Dramatic irony opens up a kind of tension between the expectations of what will occur in the story, with a character believing one thing, and the reader another. Because of this tension, dramatic irony is common in tragedies, as well as in horror stories. Mary believes Gabriel is an angel of God, whereas the reader believes that Gabriel is a space alien. This distinction is based on the reader recognizing the references to the supernatural and to science fiction. Some of the direct references are that he is from another planet, he seems to have special powers, the aliens have a spaceship, and that he uses modern scientific terminology. Mary hears these pieces of information, but she either does not understand them outside of a religious context or she does not understand what Gabriel is saying at all because the words or ideas are so foreign. The reader, however, who understands the information revealed by Gabriel will come to the reasonable conclusion that Gabriel is a space alien. One of the first somewhat comical examples of dramatic irony that is dependent on a reader recognizing certain references is the physical description of Gabriel:

> He was tall, and luminous white hair fell freely over his shoulders. His eyes sparkled red. His clothing was even odder than his physical appearance. He wore a tunic tightly fitted to his chest and fastened by a gold belt. Shoes that shone like polished bronze encased his feet. A transparent globe, similar to an aureole, surrounded his head. The stranger took the halo in his hand and gently placed it on a chair before speaking. (202)

This description of Gabriel is consistent with the traditional biblical figure of an angel. At the same time, this description is also consistent with a science fiction humanoid alien in a classic spaceman outfit. One aspect of his appearance, the space helmet, makes the description of Gabriel particularly clear as science fiction, since one cannot, after all, take a halo off.[2]

The differing beliefs of Mary and the reader, however, are not just a matter of worldview and knowledge of science fiction, but of Gabriel's lies and manipulation. The nature of the relationship between Mary and Gabriel is initially clear from Gabriel's attitude of superiority to Mary and his condescending manner of speaking to her. In one instance, when Mary is expressing how much she is attracted to him, Gabriel responds: "'Mary!' he exclaimed, moved, 'little thing'" (207). The name he calls her is clearly meant to depict her as lower than himself, even if he has affection for her. It is also significant to note that Mary's understanding of who Gabriel is and why he is visiting her cannot be solely attributed to her own religious worldview. Mary sees Gabriel as an angel precisely because he lies to her, manipulates her, and takes advantage of her misunderstanding of him as a messenger of God. This is seen in the seduction scene that follows their initial meeting:

> He held her hands and kissed them.
> "They are as soft as a dove's feathers," he said. She blushed slightly.
> "You're exaggerating. Surely, the wings of the celestial cherubs are much softer." "Cherubs?" he let slip. "Oh, yes! But don't you believe such a thing. Of course, heaven has much that is lovely, but I've never seen anything there as beautiful as your smile." (Chaviano, "Annunciation" 205)

Gabriel, somewhat comically, forgets that Mary sees him as one of the angels and makes a mistake in questioning her about the angels. The facade comes quickly back as he continues manipulating her through her own beliefs. Gabriel also spins certain aspects of the aliens' plan with regard to Joseph:

> "When must my husband know about this?" she asked him.
> "As soon as he returns. At this moment he lies asleep along the road that leads to Nazareth."
> Mary felt suddenly upset.
> "Sleeping along the road to Nazareth? Heavens!"
> "Do not be alarmed. The great Iab-eh is watching over his sleep." The young woman was calmed. (203–204)

Gabriel concludes the discussion of Joseph in a way that it seems Iab-eh is taking care of Joseph for his own benefit, whereas it is clear that the aliens are keeping Joseph asleep so that Gabriel can seduce Mary. Joseph is simply an obstacle to the aliens' overall plan. Gabriel's lies and manipulation of the truth signal that something sinister is going on.

Taking into consideration Gabriel's lies and manipulation, the sexual encounter seems more like sexual coercion than "making love," the phrase that the *Encyclopedia of Science Fiction* (s.v. "Daína Chaviano") uses as a description of the scene. In "The Annunciation," Gabriel has come to Mary to announce that she will have a child and then he proceeds to enact this plan. He has not come to ask her if it's acceptable to have a child with him. In this light, the story, though it has comedic elements, is a science fiction horror story as well, an alien seducing a young woman for the benefit of the invading powers. She is not in control of the reproductive act in which she is involved. That power is firmly in the alien hands of Gabriel. The primary horror of the story is the sexual assault and rape of Mary. It is true that not everyone will understand this situation to be sexual assault and rape, and therefore horrific, that is, this interpretation is likely dependent on a feminist political viewpoint. Given that Mary trusts Gabriel completely and is submitting to him because of religion, her capability to give consent here is almost nonexistent. Mary's fear never leaves and is only waylaid by her forced submission to Gabriel. Mary's reaction to the seduction fluctuates, and she responds at times by submissively accepting the seduction on account of Gabriel's position of authority as an angel of God, and at other times by resisting the advances of Gabriel:

> "Your dress, doesn't it bother you?"
> "Not at all!" she protested weakly.
> "But you are wearing so many things," he sighed.
> "No, I assure you. Only what you see and . . ." lowering her voice modestly, "a very light tunic beneath."
> "You should take it off. It's hot."

"The air is cool . . ."

His hands delicately undid the ties of her dress, and it fell to the floor. Mary didn't dare protest for fear of offending him. (Chaviano, "Annunciation" 206)

The implication here is that she does in fact resist Gabriel to a certain degree, even if he is able to ultimately take advantage of her submission to him. I think the best comparison, and one that is evoked by the story, is the abuse of power by a religious leader. In these cases, a religious leader convinces someone to have sex because it is God's will or something of the sort. The coercion in these cases does not happen through physical force, but through social coercion, using religion and authority as a weapon. Even still, in "The Annunciation" there is certainly the possibility of force in the background. The seduction of Mary is not physically violent, but Gabriel, as an alien, seems to have super powers as well as a mandate to impregnate Mary. If Mary were to try to physically resist, it can be assumed that she would have little chance of getting free. The expressions of sexuality, pleasure, playfulness, and mystical union do not negate the fact that Gabriel is posing as a religious authority and taking advantage of a young woman. By the same token, Gabriel's obvious enjoyment of the seduction and sex, as well as his declaration that he "loves" Mary (205), does not take away the element of sexual coercion.

That the birth of Jesus, a sacred and celebrated birth in the Christian tradition, has an element of horror is a dark irony. At the same time, it is a liberation from the chaste tradition attached to Mary, since she here experiences the pleasures of seduction, sexual pleasure, and ultimately, orgasm. The portrayal of Mary in this story is quite different from the chaste Mary of the Christian tradition. In the context of the portrayal of Mary throughout history, as Juan Carlos Toledano Redondo notes: "This fresh . . . new version of the Annunciation represents the possibility of women's enjoyment of sex by making the most pious of women enjoy it" (38). Yolanda Molina-Gavilán places the alternate view of Mary in the context of the Latin American cultural phenomenon of *marianismo*, which upholds the chaste Mary as the ideal woman: "Chaviano's version of the annunciation attacks the concept of marianismo by challenging one of its most sacred bases, Mary's sexuality" ("Eugenic Orgasms?"). The depiction of Mary as a fully sexual person is an important liberation from past portrayals of women's sexuality.

During the seduction of Mary, she is sexually aroused. She experiences desire and responds sexually to Gabriel, feeling new and surprising sensations, and even going so far as to pronounce: "I feel so good that I don't know how I could have lived all these years so far from you" (Chaviano, "Annunciation" 207). Mary also expresses a degree of playful sexual agency, as for example, when the narrator states: "She looked obediently at him. The angel of the Lord was certainly handsome" (204). The ending of the story has the two in bed without clothes, and Mary is "penetrated by an undreamed sensation of height and vertigo," and "a hot shower had bathed the deepest part of her seed" (207). The reader will recognize the sex and orgasm, but Mary also seems to be having a religious experience, a quasi-mystical sexual experience, as the narrator notes: "The door of the kingdom opened before both of them" (207). Ultimately, Mary embraces the angel in the moment of orgasm: "'Gabriel,' she grabbed him tightly by the shoulders, 'You are . . . !'" (207). The implied conclusion to the exclamation is that he is a "God," giving a powerful yet playful tone to the scene. Mary may be transformed through sexual liberation, but she is not in control of the reproductive act in which she is involved.

There is also another more cosmic aspect of horror in the story that arises from the reason for the alien's plans to impregnate Mary, made clear when Gabriel claims "Eugenics" to be guiding them: "Eugenics has never failed, and you have been chosen" (203). Mary obviously does not know that eugenics, an early twentieth-century theory and social practice, is an attempt to "improve" humanity through breeding. The reader, however, discovers through Gabriel's statements that the aliens have been watching her, presumably studying the population, to determine the best candidate for interbreeding. According to Gabriel, the aliens are intending to create a great and wise being who will become a leader of the aliens. He says that Jesus "is called to succeed the great Iab-eh on the throne towards the march to Infinity" (203). Furthermore, Jesus will serve the aliens in another way: "The fruit of this union will lead Iab-eh's spaceship to our own planet. The information must get there, and our wise men have decided upon the mixture of both races" (205). The idea of Jesus leaving the planet is a sly reference to the ascension of Jesus into heaven, and with these statements, it is known that Mary is simply a pawn in a larger cosmic purpose. The aliens want something from humanity and they are intent on getting it. At the same time, they believe themselves to be superior, and indeed, there is, as in many alien narratives, a colonial element to the alien encounter. The aliens in "The Annunciation" have come to Earth and are attempting to culturally influence the humans, all the while thinking that the natives do not understand. Gabriel says about humanity: "You haven't understood the half of our moral teachings. Instead of applying them, you've converted them into religion" (205). This is precisely the message of liberation of Jesus: that enacting the precepts of religion are more important than following the rules of religion. This liberation comes with the liberation of the space aliens because Jesus will leave the planet to bring information (possibly the genetic code of humanity) to the home planet and help them to break out of their own genetic walls. This liberation, however, is very much dependent on taking the space aliens' perspective, something that is central to understanding the next story.

As in "The Annunciation," the element of horror in Mercurio Rivera's "Dance of the Kawkawroons" from his collection *Across the Event Horizon* (2013) is also primarily accessed not by a character but through a reading structured by dramatic irony. The story is focused on the strange entanglement between humans and the Kawkawroons (Kawks, as the narrator calls them), who are giant bird-like space aliens with two intertwined consciousnesses. Although the story is focused on the humans, it is narrated by two alternating narrators, a human and the Kawkawroon he meets, thereby allowing readers a glimpse into who the Kawkawroons are from their perspective. At the time the story is set, humans and Kawkawroons have had some contact, but the humans have set up a quarantine around the Kawkawroon planet, barring humans from landing. The central plot involves the unnamed human narrator and his partner, Annie, who are given Inspiration by a friend who is a xenobiologist. Inspiration, the yolk of a Kawkawroon egg, gives the taker a strong desire to create advanced technology, and it gives them scientific knowledge and intimate knowledge about the Kawkawroons. Annie creates a human-Kawkawroon translator, and the narrator creates a cloaking device to get them past the quarantine. The pair travels to the Kawkawroon planet looking for more Inspiration. They encounter one of the Kawkawroons, and after they perform the proper dance, the Kawkawroon lays twelve eggs and offers them one. The narrator, however, shoots the Kawkawroon and they take all twelve. They make it back to Earth, where they continue to take Inspiration and begin working at the Hawaiian Xenobiology Institute. They, along with all the others in the world taking Inspiration, are planning to bring some Kawkawroons and are inventing machines that will help the Kawkawroons live on Earth.

The story begins, like many stories with a kernel of horror, with a benign image of beauty and innocence: "WINDSWEPT CONFETTI. That's how Annie had described the Kawkawroons when she first spotted them hovering miles away against the white sky, bookended by the twin suns" (11). The Kawkawroons are a beautiful blue and yellow, and other than their humanoid faces, they seem in many ways like the birds that humans know on Earth, even having migratory patterns. Eventually, however, the horror is revealed. The horror of the story is that the Kawkawroons are taking over human society, which will ultimately lead to the enslavement and then decimation of humanity. The true extent of the horror of the story can be pieced together with a number of important clues. Primarily, the entire world is engaged in great technological advances that Inspiration engenders; however, they do not yield inventions to benefit humans but the Kawkawroons. The humans, for example, have recently made "'a chemical bath that simulates the composition of their ocean so they can stay healthy and disease-free. An AI-driven communicator that allows us more nuanced interactions with them so we can follow their complex rituals and maximize egg production'" (23). The goal from the human viewpoint is to bring the Kawkawroons to Earth so that they can get more Inspiration. Although the humans seem normal, they are being controlled by what is essentially an addictive drug, and they are doing everything to get more. The horror in the story is the enslavement of humanity to work for the Kawkawroons and the tool they use is the yolk of their eggs.

The horror is not only one of human enslavement but also of the extinction of humanity. At the end of the story, as Inspiration has spread throughout the world, humans are constructing towers in many major cities, so that the Kawkawroons have a place to perch upon. This building of towers connects to another part of the story, when the narrator first describes the world of the Kawkawroons: "In the distance, the rust-red peak of a derelict tower broke the surface of the ocean. Built by a long-extinct civilization before sea levels had risen, tens of thousands of these submerged skeletal spires dotted this alien waterworld" (11). It can be surmised that the Kawkawroon planet was the home of some other species, now long dead, and the thousands of towers indicates that they had brought the Kawkawroons to their planet and built them large towers before dying out. It seems this same process is happening to humanity and the Kawkawroons will remain on Earth, whereas the humans will eventually perish. In addition, the decimation of humanity is indicated by the fact that the humans who take Inspiration are uninterested in sex, as seen when the narrator asks Annie to have sex: "but I made the half-hearted offer more out of habit than any real desire. It had been months since we'd slept together. 'I have another idea,' she said, wiggling free. And I knew immediately what she had in mind: something better than sex. 'Let me guess. Inspiration?'" (23–24). It seems that even though humans do not know exactly how Inspiration works, it compels the taker to take enormous pleasure in work and to prefer it to all else. They will simply enjoy the scientific discovery that goes along with the experience of Inspiration, with the result that the human race will eventually die out.

Putting together these pieces, the reader sees something that the narrator and Annie do not see: Inspiration is causing the enslavement and death of humanity. In fact, the humans seem to specifically be incapable of coming to the awareness that they are being manipulated by Inspiration. Inspiration directly changes their brain and stops them from thinking that they are in danger from the Kawkawroons. This mental cover-up is displayed in this scene involving the narrator and Annie:

A feeling nagged at me that I was missing something.

"So how long do you think before construction of the tower is complete?" I said.

"Not long at all," she said.

And at that moment, an image struck me. An image of countless Kawkaw-roons perched atop tens of thousands of towers across the globe, the human throngs staring up at them, blank-eyed, dancing at their feet.

"What's wrong?" she said.

I froze, struggling to retain the thought, but just like that, it disappeared like daylight behind a pulled window shade, eclipsed by a burst of sudden Inspiration.

"Nothing," I said, itching to get to work. "Nothing at all." (24)

The dance here refers to the dance that a species must do to request that the Kawkawroons give them an egg and therefore Inspiration. This image of danc-ing is not that of joyous free dancing, since they are doing it because they are being compelled to by Inspiration. The humans are "blank-eyed" meaning that they are doing it out of inner compulsion. The enslaved humans cannot get past the mental barriers put up by the Kawkawroons. The cover-up of the horror is part of the horror itself, that is, the Kawkawroons use Inspiration to cover up colonization and genocide, engaging in dissimulation to conquer humanity. What is powerful about this alien take-over is that it is done from the inside, that is, the primary mode of take-over is mental colonization and the humans do the work willingly.

As a corollary to this cover-up, the humans do not see the Kawkawroons act-ing in any aggressive or militaristic way that might tip them off. There is little evidence that the take-over is done with evil intentions or is even meant to be a take-over at all. The Kawkawroon narrator states that the moment the human narrator takes the eggs is a wonderful moment: "When the strangers crouched down and began to empty my nest, removing lifefont after lifefont, I forgot my pain and yawped with delight! Kawkawroon legend spoke of so many other strangers of different shapes and forms who had followed this same path. I did not understand it entirely, but I knew this was all part of the prophecies, part of the sacred, unknowable plan" (21–22). In this sense, the Kawkawroons are as much the victim of the biological manipulation as the humans, that is, their biology is dictating to themselves that another species become addicted to their eggs. Furthermore, not only do the humans not suspect the Kawkawroons; they believe themselves to be the ones acting aggressively. The humans are so obliv-ious to the fact that they are being colonized, that they think that humans are the ones colonizing the Kawkawroons. Annie asks the human narrator:

"Do you ever feel, I don't know, a little guilty about all this? About what we've done to the Kawks?"

"Guilty? Not really. We're treating them well." I understood what she meant, but it was just the natural order, a pattern repeated throughout human history. Cultures colliding. Conquest. Yes, we had conquered the Kawks, but it wasn't as if we'd really enslaved them." (23)

This way of thinking is ultimately beneficial to the Kawkawroons because it compels the humans to accept this situation, believing that it is natural that they are exploiting the Kawkawroons for their eggs.

On one level, it seems there is little redeeming social liberation depicted in this story. The humans will be enslaved and murdered. However, the story invites readers to take another perspective, in particular the Kawkawroon perspective. It is the humans who are being colonized, but the Kawkawroons are being liberated. This can be seen in a detail from the initial description of the world that the "sea levels had risen," indicating that there is an environmental disaster happening for the Kawkawroons, who after all need a place to land (11). The Kawkawroons are being liberated from climate change by the humans. Taking into consideration the Kawkawroon perspective, the human horror is a Kawkawroon liberation. This story makes it clear that the meeting of the humans and the Kawkawroons can be allegorically read as a first contact moment. After shooting the Kawkawroon, the narrator imagines this response to the Kawkawroon: "I'm sorry, I thought. You encountered a more advanced alien civilization and paid the price. How many species in the universe have met the same fate?" (21). As becomes clear with the rest of the story, however, the situation is reversed. In this reading, the Kawkawroons are correlated with the Native Americans and the humans are correlated with the European Americans. If we extend the allegory of colonization beyond what the human narrator is capable of and take the other perspective, we can see that the story takes a turn. This scenario is then a reversal of *The War of the Worlds* in which the invaders who are correlated with Indigenous groups are killed off by a bacteria.

In the case of "Dance of the Kawkawroons," the natives survive, and they do so through Inspiration. Allegorically, Inspiration can be read as cultural appropriation. Europeans and Americans have been taking Inspiration from Indigenous cultures and people of color for centuries, and often with violent means, as is shown in the story. There may be a sort of indirect benefit from cultural appropriation, however: over time, it may mean a continuation of culture—a passing on of culture—to take it back one day. The idea is that Europeans and Americans believe that they have an advanced civilization that makes it natural that they would conquer the Indigenous people of the Americas. They can freely take cultural elements of the colonized people at will and without having to engage the actual people in the culture. In this scenario, they are wrong. The eventual decimation of the humans, in allegorical terms, would mean that life continues for Indigenous people. What may seem like colonization is simply the seeds of destruction for the colonizer. The Kawkawroons, however, are survivors.

In these stories, the beginning of the horrors comes at the end of the story. This is important in understanding how they relate to the making of the alien consciousness in Latinx science fiction. The moment of horror in these works is a halting of the development of the alien consciousness. The aliens in these works are confronted, but they are not fully embraced. There are real human limits to the making of the alien consciousness, to holding intact the vision of a radically inclusive society. At the same time, such experiences of horror over time do result in a liberation that will one day lead to a greater alien consciousness. There is, ironically, great hope in these stories. In the next chapter, we take a further step, offering an alternative to the alien consciousness that arises with the Chupacabras, that most infamous of Latinx space aliens.

7

La conciencia Chupacabras

■■■■■■■■■■■■■■■■■■■■■

Gloria Anzaldúa's concept of the alien consciousness is vital for envisioning a future for Latinx communities. There is an alternative vision, however: *la conciencia Chupacabras*, which gives counterbalance to the utopian sensibility of the alien consciousness by focusing on the present-day threats to Latinx communities rather than future triumphs. The Chupacabras phenomenon started in 1995 in Puerto Rico, beginning with numerous reports of the exsanguination and deaths of farm animals. After these animal killings and the various sightings of an elusive creature, the events coalesced in the media under the name el Chupacabras, a term that seems to have been coined by the comedian Silverio Pérez (qtd. in Román 198). The mysterious nature of the Chupacabras created a dialogue, an interchange of multiple interpretations about what the Chupacabras is and why it is significant. Out of the dialogue, *la conciencia Chupacabras* is born, as Puerto Rico constructed and confronted a new cultural figure. *La conciencia Chupacabras* has many of the key aspects of the alien consciousness, given that the Chupacabras is often described as a space alien itself; in particular, it is a vision of radical inclusivity, as well as being tolerant of ambiguity and perplexity. However, this stance does not result in a synthesis or a mixture of the "best" of all the cultures as does the alien consciousness; rather, it remains fixed in an unending state of ambiguity, and at times expresses a tense and frightening sensibility.

La conciencia Chupacabras should be seen in the context of the long-standing connection between Puerto Rico and space aliens. This connection began in earnest in the 1960s when the Arecibo Observatory and radio telescope was constructed in Puerto Rico under the control of Cornell University. The observatory, which houses one of the world's largest radio telescopes, analyzes radio waves from space to study the universe. Radio waves, of course, are also a means of communication. This meant that the observatory became a focus for thinking about radio communications with beings from outer space, also known as SETI (the search for extraterrestrial intelligence). James Gunn's novel *The Listeners* (1972), for example, tells the story of the receipt of an alien message by the observatory and its political fallout. The connection between Arecibo and space aliens was cemented on November 16, 1974, when the observatory transmitted the first human message into space that was specifically designed for space aliens. The Arecibo message, if interpreted correctly by extraterrestrials, will result in a pictorial diagram showing the numbers one through ten, some basic scientific information, an image of a human, and the Arecibo telescope itself. Since the message was sent to a cluster of stars twenty-five thousand light years away, it is not likely that we will receive an answer any time soon, if at all ("The Arecibo Message" 462). The idea of a response, however, continues to fascinate: if Puerto Rico was sending messages, then Puerto Rico might be the place to receive the response.

The connection between Puerto Rico and space aliens appeared with a Chupacabras-like phenomenon not long after the Arecibo Message was sent, when a number of animal killings were reported in 1975 in the town of Moca. Although the killings were later revealed as a plot to devalue a farmer's land, there were numerous fantastic interpretations of the events. The eyewitnesses of the culprit described the creature as an enormous bird or a bat, and named it el vampiro de Moca. Numerous witnesses also saw UFOs at the time, which they connected to el vampiro (Román 211–213). The connection Puerto Rico has to the space alien continued to appear in fiction as well, and the observatory was the setting for a number of science fiction narratives such as Carl Sagan's novel *Contact* (1985), which was inspired by *The Listeners*, as well as the film *Species* (1995).[1] One prominent example was *The X-Files* episode "Little Green Men" (S2E1), which appeared in September 1994 and is set at the observatory. The premise of "Little Green Men" is that aliens have received the message sent out into space at Arecibo and that they are responding. Mulder is desperate for evidence of the existence of space aliens, and he comes to the observatory to retrieve the computer recordings of the event. At the observatory, Mulder meets Jorge, the Puerto Rican caretaker of the observatory. Jorge is depicted as childlike and unfamiliar with the technology in the observatory, evidenced when Mulder chides him for touching a button on the computer. In this way, the show is consistent with the other science fiction depictions of Arecibo, as well as the actual history of the observatory, that it is not the Puerto Ricans who control the observatory, but the Americans.[2] When the space aliens appear and Jorge dies, seemingly from being frightened to death, he becomes valuable to Mulder as mere physical evidence, with Mulder reprehensibly even suggesting that they ship him back to FBI headquarters. It is as if Mulder suggests that Jorge be abducted. There is a sense that the aliens have invaded Puerto Rico, but these aliens are not from outer space.

Not long after Mulder showed up in Puerto Rico, the Chupacabras was born, and it was born as a Multitude. The mystery of the animal killings induced numerous theories. There were naturalist explanations such as the idea that the Chupacabras is a predator such as a mongoose or snake. There was the crypto-zoologist explanation that the Chupacabras is a cryptid, an undiscovered creature such as Sasquatch or the Loch Ness Monster. Others claimed the creature was a devil or demon, while still others considered the entire situation a joke. Also prominent are the science fiction accounts that the creature was a medical experiment from a secret American military base in El Yunque gone awry, and most important, for this book, the Chupacabras is typically considered to be of extraterrestrial origin. These multiple interpretations are not free-floating theories but are enmeshed in the complexities of institutional power.

The mystery of the Chupacabras and its many interpretations birthed a complex interplay between rural social structures, governmental bodies, the media, religions, universities, and various other institutions in Puerto Rico. Reinaldo L. Román describes the political situation: "The . . . chupacabras exposed afflictions plaguing Puerto Ricans in their dealings with federal and commonwealth government officials. But these narratives of occult depredations were the stuff of spectacle-making and satire, too. Crowds gathered at killing sites to steal a glimpse of the monsters, make demands of officials, and participate in the vacilón" (213; *vacilón* can be roughly translated as a back and forth ribaldry). The Chupacabras was serious business as well as performative politics. Because the Chupacabras could not be easily integrated into any accepted system of control, it took on a populist quality. The very uniqueness of the Chupacabras laid bare the contours of political life, as politicians could not rely on well-worn responses. The result is that the "chupacabras discourses authorized allegedly credulous citizens to speak for themselves" (213). The mystery of the Chupacabras called into being a contentious and yet lighthearted dialogue that continues today.[3]

After its birth in 1995, the Chupacabras was in continual dialogue with science fiction. The traditional image of the Chupacabras, though differently described by many witnesses, was primarily formed through an encounter reported by Madelyne Tolentino in August 1995. Tolentino described the creature as around four-feet tall, with large ovoid eyes, three-fingered claws, and spikes up and down its spine. In a 1996 interview, Tolentino notes that the interviewer should watch the space alien film *Species* (1995) to get a good idea about what the Chupacabras looks like, and to see a depiction of its origin story, which entails that it is both from outer space and the product of a government experiment. Tolentino also importantly notes in her interview the connection between space aliens and Puerto Rico, commenting on the surprising fact that the film begins at the Arecibo Observatory (Corrales 31–59). In *Tracking the Chupacabra*, Benjamin Radford, noting that the film came out just prior to Tolentino's sighting, takes a skeptical stance regarding Tolentino's report, arguing that she most likely confabulated whatever she saw with the space alien from the film *Species* (137). Whatever the order of causation regarding the description of the Chupacabras, from its beginnings, the Chupacabras was intertwined in dialogue with the language of science fiction. Eventually, Tolentino's space alien Chupacabras became the dominant description of what the Chupacabras looks like.

After becoming a media phenomenon in Puerto Rico, this creature crossed borders into the mainland United States, Mexico, and Latin America as a whole. The populism of the Chupacabras, as well as its Spanish-language name, which marked it as a Latinx creature, enabled it to reach its claws into the wider Latinx world. The initial migration was in part a result of the burgeoning internet, but it was also conveyed through Spanish-language television shows, in particular *Cristina*, which did a story on the Chupacabras in March 1996 (Radford 10). The Chupacabras then transformed into a contemporary folktale figure in Latin America, where it found fertile ground in struggling rural communities, and eventually it transformed into a doglike creature, the subject of cryptozoologists in Texas and the American Southwest. The Chupacabras is a mystery, and this mystery encourages people to offer interpretations lacking in evidence. The result is a proliferation of opinions. The meaning of the Chupacabras in each locale is different, and one of the most significant aspects of the creature is its ability to form dialogue across national borders and express threats to Latinx communities from Puerto Rico to Mexico to Argentina.

Lauren Derby writes that the Chupacabras in Puerto Rico is "more a post-Cold War glimpse of the face of American imperialism as it looks from the backstage of empire, in the eyes of those who want nothing more than to be on the other side of the curtain" (312). William Calvo-Quirós connects the Chupacabras to the threats of late capitalism: "The Chupacabras thus emerges as a sophisticated epistemic product rendering visible the invisible economic polices whose deadly effects were being felt in vulnerable communities" (51). Calvo-Quirós also points to Rudolfo Anaya's young-adult novel *The Curse of the ChupaCabra* and its correlation of poverty and drug abuse with the Chupacabras. The Chupacabras is working in a pan-Latinx context and its ability to foster dialogue has traveled from Puerto Rico to the rest of Latin America.

The multiplicity of meanings connected to the Chupacabras is present in many of its cultural expressions and it appeared in one of the Chupacabras's most widespread manifestations in *The X-Files*. "El Mundo Gira" (S4E11) aired in January 1997, demonstrating the rapid journey of the Chupacabras from Puerto Rico a year and a half earlier. The story is centered on a group of undocumented workers in the San Joaquin Valley of California. True to the title of the show, which translates to "As the World Turns," there is a love triangle comprised of two brothers, Eladio and Soledad, who are both in love with Maria, the wife of Soledad. One morning, under clear skies, there is a blinding light followed by a yellow rain falling onto the camp. Maria and Eladio are walking together out in the open, but only Maria is killed by the yellow rain. Eladio survives and seems to have somehow soaked up the yellow rain. He goes on the run, fearing that people will think he killed Maria. Instead of dying, he develops some strange symptoms: he is first sweaty and pale and then begins to leak yellow slime, he gets pustules on his face, and when he touches someone they die, seemingly eaten by a fungus. With the help of Immigration and Naturalization Service agent Lozano, played by Rubén Blades, Mulder and Scully investigate the death of Maria. Ultimately, Eladio's face and head are distorted to the point that he looks something like the typical gray alien, and he and his brother, who has also been transformed, get away, headed for Mexico.

The ambiguity concerning what the Chupacabras was in Puerto Rico traveled with the figure and was translated into the literary or filmic device of narrative ambiguity, in which there are questions or gaps in knowledge in the story, with the story providing multiple answers without finally determining which one of them is right. The first answer to the question of what happened to Eladio comes from within the migrant worker community and is offered by Flakkita, the initial narrator of the show, who believes that Eladio is the Chupacabras and that he killed Maria. The second explanation is the very human telenovela plot line, which claims that Eladio killed Maria because she didn't love him. This is the view supported by the brother Soledad, at least initially, and it causes him to pursue Eladio to enact vengeance. The third explanation is Scully's scientific explanation. This explanation initially takes the form of claiming that Maria and Eladio are the victims of farm pesticides, in particular methyl bromide, which Scully finds in Maria's blood. After more testing, however, Scully determines that Maria and the people killed by Eladio's touch contain a strange enzyme that causes a fungus (common athlete's foot) to rapidly reproduce and overtake its victim. Maria was the victim of this fungus-catalyzing enzyme, but Eladio became a carrier because he had some immunity to the enzyme. The fourth explanation, Mulder's extraterrestrial explanation, is that while the effects of the fungus are entirely mundane, the origin of the enzyme is outer space.

The show never states clearly which of the explanations is correct, as each explanation has some evidence of truth. The narrative ambiguity of the show, which places truth on shaky ground, is heightened by the multiple narrators of the show. The show is initially framed by the storytelling of Flakkita, who is in the dark, with candles, saying: "Quiet! Quiet, listen to me. It was a terrible thing. You're not going to believe me, even when I tell you. Some say it is a story, a fairy tale. But I saw it. I saw it with my own eyes." At the end of the show, however, two other storytellers enter as well, Gabrielle, the friend of Eladio who is telling the tale of the Chupacabras to a group of workers, and Mulder and Scully, who are reporting to their boss, Walter Skinner. Their conclusion sums up the situation:

SKINNER: Frankly, I'm confused by this story.
MULDER: I don't blame you.
SCULLY: We can't exactly explain it ourselves, sir.

The ambiguity of the truth of the events in the show mirrors the ambiguity of how the show deals with the politics of immigration. The show was originally aired in January, 1997, while California's Proposition 187 and its harsh stance on immigration was being debated. In the show, there is a strong correlation between immigrants and space aliens, and Scully supports the liberal perspective on immigration, as when he says: "Mulder, I know you don't want to hear this, but I think the aliens in this story are not the villains. They're the victims." The show does offer a sympathetic view of the migrant workers, who are shown to be hard working and honorable, and demonstrates that they are not really the cause of the problem but are simply the victims and the carriers of a disease caused by others. Even though the show tries to show that the aliens are not the villains, however, the basic pattern of threat and victimhood that is common in science fiction remains. Ultimately, "El Mundo Gira" presents the general ambiguous liberal version of the going alien narrative: as humans, Latinxs are not a threat, and in fact they are the victims, as Scully states, but as space aliens they are a monstrous threat to the nation. Even with a non–Latinx-produced show, the Chupacabras was imported with its inherent multiplicity intact.

After the airing of "El Mundo Gira," the correlation between the Chupacabras and Mexican migrants became its most common allegorical connection. As was the case at its beginnings in Puerto Rico, the Chupacabras almost always appears with a hint of humor amidst the blood and fear. A plethora of B-movie horror films about the Chupacabras appeared that drew on the idea of a "Latino" monster in the United States, although a handful are interesting in their inclusion of Chicanx characters. In *Mexican Werewolf in Texas* (2005), a racist White father dresses as the Chupacabras to scare his daughter's Chicano boyfriend. Writing about this film, Jesse Alemán demonstrates that the film's racial politics are uneven in its critique of racism since it maintains female White supremacy (55). In *Chupacabra vs. the Alamo* (2013) starring Erik Estrada, the Battle of the Alamo is refought, but this time with Anglos and Mexicans joined together. Both films correlate the Chupacabras with contemporary Mexican immigrants, and generally in a negative way. The byline of *Mexican Werewolf in Texas* warns: "Terror has JUST crossed the border!" In the hands of Latinx writers and artists, however, the Chupacabras has the capacity to be correlated with a variety of figures or threats to Latinx communities. The metaphor of the Chupacabras as immigrant is present in Juan Manuel Perez's poem "Open Letter from the Chupacabra," in which the Chupacabras is compared to a misunderstood undocumented immigrant just trying to survive. This time, however, there is little ambiguity about its politics of immigration:

> "Since when is it a crime to eat, feast
> Just to survive, just to be hunted down
> Like some innocent, illegal immigrant"
> "I will not die, I will not live in fear
> No bullet from your barrel will touch me
> I will be like the ghost you cannot hold
> Like the phantasm that remains unclear
> I will have you on the run from your own
>   insecurities"
> "You will perish with your insanity
> Like those that find false many other Mexican truths:
> *La Virgen De Guadalupe, La Llorona, La Lechusa*
> All silent victims to your nativistic biases"

The idea is that undocumented immigrants may be perceived as a threat, but they are innocent, just as the Chupacabras. The primary point of connection made between the Chupacabras and immigrants is that they are being "hunted down," not that they are threatening creatures. The real threat is the hunter, the Anglos, with their guns, their nativism, and their lack of respect for Mexican beliefs and culture. In addition, there is a pretty clear expression of the Reappropriation of the Invading Space Alien technique, as the Chupacabras promises to haunt the hunters and "have you on the run from your own insecurities." The Chupacabras is correlated with the migrant, but it is fierce in its defense of *la cultura*. In this way, the Chupacabras is more of an antihero than a hero.[4]

With his short story collection *Chupacabra Vengeance* (2017), David Bowles took the Chupacabras in many ways back to its roots as a monster attacking Latinx communities. In these stories, the Chupacabras is just one more threat added to the many threats to migrants as they cross the border, and the political oppression experienced by Chicanxs in the United States. In an online prologue to the collection, "Chupacabra Genesis," Bowles offers a fascinating origin story for the Chupacabras in which flying saucers landed on Earth and released nanobots into the world that then take over living beings, turning them into killing machines. Two Chupacabras stories are set in this background. In "Aztlán Liberated," a group of Chicanxs destroy the Chupacabras queen and make the ultimate sacrifice for their patria. In "Chupacabra Vengeance," a migrant girl is pursued by a raging hoard of Chupacabras but has an uncanny connection to them nevertheless. In both cases, however, the strength of the Chupacabras is matched by the bravery and spirit of the Latinx characters. It is important to note that in his poem "Chupacabra Genesis" Bowles also points to the actual origin of the Chupacabras in Puerto Rico, bringing the creature full-circle home:

> In the morning, as cousins on a distant isle
> have already done, the troop leaves goats drained.
> All day they sleep, dreaming a singular dream,
> A portent of the future—the queen is on her way.

In 2006, the Chupacabras returned to Puerto Rico with Tato Laviera's "Puerto Rico's Chupacabras." This poem expresses the great capacity of the Chupacabras to bring a disparate community together, not under a national flag but through a lively dialogue. The poem is included in Laviera's collection *Mixturao and Other Poems* (2008) and it comes somewhat late in Laviera's career, following iconic works such as *La Carreta Made a U-Turn* in 1979 and *AmeRícan* in 1985, both of which affirmed the unique and complex experience of Puerto Ricans in the United States. The poem shows Laviera's continued dedication to finding new images that express the collective experience of being Puerto Rican. Given that by the publication of Laviera's poem in 2006 the Chupacabras had already become fixed as a pan-Latinx creature, the title of the poem is significant. Laviera says in an interview with William Luis: "I live for the title. I am a title poet. The words of the title are the ultimate essence, and the background of my writing is to bring the title to its most total development" (1025). In this case, the title indicates that the Chupacabras is of Puerto Rican heritage and distinguishes Puerto Rico's Chupacabras from the Chupacabras from the United States and the rest of Latin America. This distinction is important because the Chupacabras, primarily because of *The X-Files*, has been somewhat disconnected from Puerto Rico in the popular imagination in the United States.

The poem is explicitly structured as a dialogue of a group of Puerto Ricans called the "milky way council of strange phenomenon," who are reporting from one of Jupiter's moons (13). It begins with the "official" statement of the council confirming that the Chupacabras is an extraterrestrial, in this case birthed from an exploding comet: "Ionosférico platillo volador radio/ Signals linked Arecibo's Sinkhole/ Observatory se estalló un cometa/ Giving birth to an extra-terrestrial" (13; Ionospheric flying saucer radio/ Signals linked Arecibo's Sinkhole/ Observatory a comet exploded/ Giving birth to an extra-terrestrial). In the rest of the poem, each stanza expresses a different member's explanation of the Chupacabras. Each stanza typically begins with the speaker addressing the group in some way, often expressing disagreement with the previous speaker's interpretation. There are fifteen such stanzas, each in quotations, and although a summary list is somewhat difficult given that the descriptions are immersed in a collage of images, it goes like this: The Chupacabras is a ghost born of disgruntled coquis (iconic frog in Puerto Rico), a satanic chemical residue, a hallucination born of Puerto Rico's political problems, an Independence Movement, an FBI agent, a powerful Halloween drink, the mascot of an extraterrestrial sports team, an imperialist joke advertising a new drink served by unemployed *piragüeros* (sellers of shaved ice), the revenge of the Pitirre (a plucky gray kingbird), the wandering spirit of *el jíbaro* (Puerto Rican farmer from the mountains), it doesn't exist, it is a new Disney character, it is a sign of the End Times, and finally, a Nuyorican street vendor selling bolitas and photos claims to be the illegitimate nephew of the Chupacabras. In the last stanza of the poem, the council comes to a comedic conclusion: "finalmente llegamos a la conclusión que el chupacabras es el espíritu de toño bicicleta protected from the authorities by the puerto rican nation" (16; finally we came to the conclusion that the Chupacabras is the spirit of Toño Bicicleta protected from the authorities by the Puerto Rican nation). As is clear from this list, the elements connected to the Chupacabras make this depiction deeply and specifically connected to Puerto Rico.

The Chupacabras, true to its origins as a killer, is described by a number of members as a representation of direct and physical threats to Puerto Ricans, such as the FBI agent (14) or the chemical residue (13). These threats can also be cultural, as seen with the corporations that are exploiting the people, such as the Disney character (16) or the drinks (14–15). At other times, the Chupacabras is more of a lighthearted expression of the frustration on the island, for example, that it is the result of the discontent of the Coquis (13) or the Pitirre (15). Then there are the views that the Chupacabras is no threat at all, as expressed by the one open skeptic of the group, as well as the one person who claims that the Chupacabras is the spirit of *el jíbaro* and "no hay más ná" (15; and nothing else). As this latter image indicates, however, there is also some affection for the Chupacabras, in part simply because it is a Puerto Rican icon. This sort of conflicted figure that is both feared and loved comes to a head with the final image of the Chupacabras as the spirit of Toño Bicicleta, the infamous outlaw of Puerto Rico who committed murders, rapes, and kidnappings. Like the criminal celebrities Bonnie and Clyde in the United States, he was exploited by the media, even while being feared and admired by the public for his rebellious charm. The connection that the space council makes between the Chupacabras and Toño Bicicleta is convincing in that they are both quasi-beloved dangers that are uniquely Puerto Rican. As an added poetic element of the connection, Toño Bicicleta was finally caught and killed by the police in 1995, the same year that the Chupacabras was born. It is as if "el espíritu de toño bicicleta" (the spirit of Toño Bicicleta) passed from his body to that of the ravaging Chupacabras (16). The Chupacabras is often seen as a threat, but he is also a Puerto Rican antihero, similar to the Chupacabras as antihero in Juan Manuel Perez's poem "Open Letter from the Chupacabra" (2015).

The final stanza of "Puerto Rico's Chupacabras" also contains some ideas about the greater significance of the Chupacabras beyond it being a threat. The text says: "lo que habiamos percibido que puerto rico es 100 × 35 × 1000" (16; what we have realized is that Puerto Rico is 100 × 35 × 1000). The colloquial way of describing the dimensions of the island is that it is 100 miles long and 35 miles wide. Adding the 1,000 to the dimensions gives the dimension of depth, indicating that Puerto Rico has a deep cultural wellspring, deeper than it is commonly believed to be, even reaching into the Nuyorican diaspora. Puerto Rico is not a static culture; from its depths, new and fascinating cultural elements are constantly being born within the existing culture. The text then states, "historias chupacabra folktales breeding creatively nuestras mitologias" (16; Chupacabras legends folktales breeding creatively our mythologies). With his invented descriptions and comedic meanings of the Chupacabras, Laviera points to the fact that there are actually many opinions about what the Chupacabras is, and that the Chupacabras offers a forum to express various political, philosophical, and cultural perspectives about being Puerto Rican. The Chupacabras takes the experiences and mythologies of Puerto Rico and multiples them, giving them new creative forms. The Chupacabras can provide a common ground for Puerto Ricans, one that is not well worn, traditional, or nationalist. This is the power of the Chupacabras, a figure that unites Puerto Ricans in a new and creative dialogue as it develops *la conciencia Chupacabras*.

La conciencia Chupacabras arises from the dialogues of a pan-Latinx context; nevertheless, the Chupacabras is not exactly a figure of pan-Latinx solidarity, and at times it even expresses some of the tensions between Latinx communities. The Chupacabras is too bloody for utopias and solidarity. The Chupacabras has a particular importance to Puerto Rico, but it is a dramatic demonstration of the Multitude of the space alien, a Multitude that is never really unified. As the Chupacabras journeyed from its birthplace in Puerto Rico to the rest of the world, it not only left dead goats in its wake, it also brought a trail of multiple interpretations and a dialogue about where it came from and what it is. There is no one thing that is the Chupacabras. What does remain is the strange dialogues, the jokes, the localized cultural expressions, and *la conciencia Chupacabras*, with its interchange of science, science fiction, popular culture, and Latinx communities.

Conclusion

■■■■■■■■■■■■■■■■■■■■■■

Fight the Future

The catch phrase "Fight the Future" from *The X-Files* is a call to resist the alien invasion being ushered in by a rich and powerful cabal. The "future" in this case is a future designed rather than unfolded, and it is singular rather than multiple. The way that *The X-Files* envisions fighting the future, however, is also bound to the designed and singular science fiction legacy of the going alien narrative. Like *The War of the Worlds*, *The X-Files* mythology is founded on a reversal of colonization, as noted by Elspeth Kydd: "*The X-Files* . . . represents a reversal of the power axis whereby Europeans and European-Americans are the primary potential victims of colonizing forces" (72). Rather than the White Americans and Europeans invading Native American lands, the space aliens are invading White America. The going alien narrative makes White America into the victim, and so the villains behind the scenes are the non-Whites. Like *The War of the Worlds*, in *The X-Files*, the space aliens are overtly tied to hegemonic colonizers, but at the same time they are tied to people of color, Indigenous groups, and immigrants. The aliens of *The X-Files* make it clear that it is a diverse future that is being fought.

Latinx science fiction writers are fighting the future on a different front, offering new futures that diverge from the going alien narratives so common in science fiction. They express variations on Gloria Anzaldúa's alien consciousness, and they depict complex yet powerful migrants, enlightened yet unbearable philosophies, and horrors that promise liberation. They depict aliens with a utopian sensibility as well as aliens who represent the violence and threats to Latinx communities. The multiplicity of the space alien enables it to play a balancing function, pointing obliquely towards Latinx solidarity. Latinx science fiction writers give complex depictions of *latinidad* as they embrace multiple futures through the Multitude of the space alien. To fight the singular future designed by racism and xenophobia, a diversity of future visions needs to be sustained, and we need to nurture in our youth the creativity needed to form those visions. Actor Edward James Olmos, who played Admiral William Adama on the television show *Battlestar Galactica*, expresses his vision in an interview about his role in the show:

> I'd say about a year after we started the program, we were into the first season . . . and a great writer . . . calls me and she's crying on the phone. She goes "hey I just want to tell you this . . . well my nephew just called me, he's twelve-years old, and he called just so happy, he was crying with joy, he says 'we're in the future, we're in the future. I saw, I saw us in the future. I saw Battlestar Galactica, and we're in the future.'" ("Battlestar Galactica—Latinos in Sci Fi")

The boy on the phone not only sees that Latinxs will be a part of the future of humanity, but also that Latinxs will be there, in space, taking part in what will be a remarkable technological transformation of humanity, into what poet Carl Marcum calls "a space-faring people" (237). The multiplication of these future visions for Latinx communities is the calling of Latinx science fiction writers.

Anzaldúa's alien consciousness as discussed in *Borderlands/La Frontera* can itself be expanded to a multiplicity of futures. One of the greatest values of the alien consciousness is its flexibility, as we continually ask, Who or what is not now included? I think the current answer to this question is the larger environment, and that the next step in the making of the alien consciousness is the embracing of the planet. Humanity is on a direct course to make the planet uninhabitable through our use of fossil fuels rather than solar, wind, and water-power. The sucking of fossil fuels from the Earth is a planetary Chupacabras, a grave threat to humanity that is made possible by our collective denial. The blunt truth is that the future of humanity depends on creating a sustainable environment for human life, and only humanity can take responsibility for the health of our home. There will be no alien consciousness if we destroy our planet. The resolution of this problem depends on our developing cosmic perception.

The history of humanity has been the story of the enlargement of our perception of our environment. Once we believed our little part of the planet was the totality of all that existed, and now we know we are part of a vast universe filled with billions and billions of stars and planets. In truth, we are not just children of Earth. We are children of the universe. From this universe-wide point of view, there are no space aliens, that is, all beings in the universe are native. Humans and other life forms in the universe share a common history—not a biological history but a cosmic-evolutionary history going back to the big bang some 13.8 billion years ago. When *los extraterrestres* show up at our door, will we even have a planet left to host them? The universe-wide perspective is an alien consciousness that will help us survive, one that embraces all that is alien, even actual space aliens. For this perspective to take hold, however, we need the fictional space alien, because the space alien demonstrates the possibility of an alien consciousness now, not in some distant future. Let us call the universe not Space but our Home.

Acknowledgments

I am grateful to so many people who have listened to my obsession with space aliens, race, and migration. Here's the short list. My work on Latinx science fiction began in earnest in a class on immigration with Ilan Stavans, to whom I will always be grateful for giving me the freedom to explore this undertheorized topic. My mentors at the University of Massachusetts Amherst, David Lenson, Jim Hicks, Laszlo Dienes, and Mario Ontiveros, supported me in a project that provoked skepticism in most people. This book could not have been written at the time I was writing my dissertation because most of the works discussed in it were published after my research was completed. There were simply not enough Latinx space alien figures before to complete a study on Latinx space aliens. I am therefore deeply in debt to the authors of *Latinx Rising: An Anthology of Latinx Science Fiction and Fantasy* (2020) who wrote some of the stories in this book. They not only supported the making of the book but have become friends as well. Frederick Luis Aldama, in particular, came into the project with an open heart, ready to begin a fruitful collaboration. Sarah Rafael Garcia and Alex Hernandez, the coeditors of my most recent editing project, *Speculative Fiction for Dreamers* (forthcoming 2021), brought to this work the refreshing experience of having like-minded people around, making editing a joy not a job. Nicole Solano, my editor at Rutgers University Press, as well as the press's readers, have been amazingly patient and supportive as I worked out the ideas of my book. This book would not have grown into what it is without the many hours discussing Latinx science fiction with my students at the University of Puerto Rico at Cayey. They are some of the brightest students I have ever encountered, and I will always appreciate their openness. With help from Isar Godreau Santiago, Mariluz Franco Ortiz, and the rest of the Interdisciplinary Institute at Cayey, and my colleagues in the Department of English, I was able to steal a couple of hours a week to work on this project.

I was also able to spend some time at the University of Chicago, where Tiana Pyer-Pereira and Edgar Garcia helped to make my stay productive. Special thanks to Lalo Alcaraz and Laura Molina, who generously agreed to have their beautiful work included in this book. Latinx science fiction has been a pretty all-consuming interest, such that my family and friends have been inundated with the topic over the years. Most recently, a number of good friends have listened to me talk about my work on Latinx science fiction and have offered valuable comments: Joseph, Erin, Obie, Patrick, James. Pablo Brescia, Jonathan Davis-Secord, and Jesse Alemán each gave detailed and book-changing comments. My family has offered amazing support through the process in all of their various ways. Mom and Dad, Whit, Gale, Isabella, Joseph, Ben, Erin, EJ, Willy, Betty, Francis, Ramon, Daniella, Emil, Valentina, Jose, Ana, Carlo, Rebecca. And as in all things, this book is dedicated to Nahir, Violet, and Enora. Without them, it just wouldn't have worked.

Notes

Introduction

1   Rachel Haywood Ferreira has, for example, examined some of the most influential works of science fiction, primarily from the nineteenth century, in her study *The Emergence of Latin American Science Fiction* (2011). The collection of essays *Latin American Science Fiction: Theory and Practice* (2012), edited by J. Andrew Brown and M. Elizabeth Ginway, explores more recent works of fiction and film. The most commonly used bibliography is Darrell B. Lockhart's *Latin American Science Fiction Writers: An A-to-Z Guide* (2003), and the most representative anthology is *Cosmos Latinos: An anthology of Science Fiction from Latin America and Spain* (2004), edited by Andrea L. Bell and Yolanda Molina-Gavilán.

2   Although I do discuss Lalo Alcaraz's graphic art in chapter 3, I do not treat art in general. For more information on science fiction art, see *Mundos Alternos: Art and Science Fiction in the Americas* (2017), an art book that accompanied a University of California, Riverside exhibit. For a study of the Latinx superheroes, see *Latinx Superheroes in Mainstream Comics* by Frederick Luis Aldama (2017).

3   Science fiction, for the purposes of this study, refers to literature or art that creates new scenarios that are in some way scientifically possible according to the science of the day. This rough-and-ready description of science fiction is meant to be somewhat ambiguous. In my mind, it is always better to have broad categories because the most interesting literature lies on the borderlines of genres.

4   According to my records of the quantity of published Latinx science fiction, there are approximately twenty-five novels and fifty short stories, along with a handful of plays and poems, not including young adult fiction, films, and comics. Relative to the entire field of science fiction, this may be quite small, but it is growing rapidly. In terms of the field of Latinx literature, one marker is that there are no works of science fiction literature in *The Norton Anthology of Latino Literature* (2011); however, the anthology does contain a science fiction image by Lalo Alcaraz, which will be discussed in chapter 3.

5   For further discussion on the role of Luis Senarens in the history of Latinx science fiction, see my essay "The Technology of Labor, Migration, and Protest" in *The Routledge Companion to Latina/o Popular Culture* (2016).

6 I am aware of two majors exceptions: Catherine Ramírez's essay "Cyborg Feminism: The Science Fiction of Octavia E. Butler and Gloria Anzaldúa," in *Reload: Rethinking Women + Cyberculture*, edited by Mary Flanagan and Austin Booth (2002), and Susana Ramírez's "Recovering Gloria Anzaldúa's Sci-Fi roots: Nepantler@ Visions in the Unpublished and Published Speculative Precursors to Borderlands," in *Altermundos: Latin@ Speculative Literature, Film, and Popular Culture*, edited by Cathryn Josefina Merla-Watson and B. V. Olguín (2017).

7 Pachucos/as were Mexican Americans who developed a unique stylized city lifestyle in the mid-twentieth century. They typically wore zoot suits and were often at odds with Anglo culture and norms. Another story centered on pachuco culture is Reyes Cárdenas's *Los Pachucos and La Flying Saucer* (1975), which involves a female UFO. This novella is more in the picaresque vein and also has a surrealist bent as the story moves from the Battle of the Alamo to the Zoot Suit Riots, and finally, to Mars.

8 *The X-Files* (1993–2002; 2016–2018) features two agents of the FBI (Federal Bureau of Investigation), Fox Mulder and Dana Scully, in their quest to discover the truth about strange, paranormal, and unexplained cases. The threats depicted in the series include such figures as vampires, ghosts, werewolves, artificial intelligence, and telepaths, but the reoccurring threat of the series is the space aliens.

Chapter 1   On Space Aliens

1 My critique of reading the space alien as the "Other" is comparable to the critique that Toni Morrison has of the use of the metaphor of invisibility by Ralph Ellison, that it is based on the assumption that it is the White community that confers visibility. The idea is to avoid when possible scholarly frameworks that center the White gaze. In other words, one can define one's own significance, especially when the other has devalued one's significance. See Als, "Ghosts in the House" (Morrison qtd.).

2 For an expanded discussion of allegory, how it is constructed, and its value as an interpretive method see my PhD dissertation, "The Fusion of Migration and Science Fiction in Mexico, Puerto Rico, and the United States" (2013). Some basic points, however, are that allegorical interpretations are based on an inductive rather than a deductive interpretive process, and so they are better understood as stronger or weaker rather than true or false, and that the specific references must be provided to make a strong interpretation.

3 Darko Suvin emphasizes that two worlds are a central component not just of the space alien but of science fiction as a whole. Furthermore, Suvin observes that two devices generally create the two worlds: "a *voyage* to a new locus, and a *catalyzer* transforming the author's environment to a new locus" (71, emphasis in the original).

4 Huhndorf demonstrates that the going native narrative was not only present in the works of writers such as Conrad and Kipling but was also a cultural logic. Huhndorf, for example, examines how world fairs such as the World's Columbian Exposition of 1893 and the living exhibitions of Indians were forms of going native since they appropriated Native American culture to establish and renew American identity (35–64).

Chapter 2   Gloria Anzaldúa and the Making of an Alien Consciousness

1   Chela Sandoval notes: "Anzaldúa was an inventor, a lover of technology, science, physics, M- and string theory. We shared a fascination with science fiction and horror" ("Foreword: Unfinished Words" xv). In an interview with her sister Hilda, it is reported: "Gloria would return to California with videotapes of science fiction shows that Hilda recorded. Her favorite had always been Star Trek and she also enjoyed Stargate SG-1 and the X-Files" (qtd. in García Ordaz, "A Writer's Legacy"). Her interest in *The X-Files* is evident in her archive at the University of Texas Austin, which contains a fan magazine and other articles about *The X-Files*. See Gloria Evangelina Anzaldúa Papers, Benson Latin American Collection, University of Texas Libraries, University of Texas at Austin, April 1980, Box 170, Folder 17.

2   The basic plot of *Alien* is that a space-mining vessel receives a distress signal from an alien planet, and when the crew lands they discover a field of space alien eggs, one of which attaches to one of the crew. The alien gestates inside him, punctures its way out, and kills the rest of the crew, except the heroine, the new science fiction feminist icon Sigourney Weaver. In many ways, it is not surprising that Anzaldúa responded strongly to this particular film because of its overt treatment of race, class, sexuality, and gender.

3   See Gloria Evangelina Anzaldúa Papers, Benson Latin American Collection, University of Texas Libraries, University of Texas at Austin, December 1996, Box 85, Folder 7. In my quotations, I retain Anzaldúa's editing marks.

4   In "Metaphors of a Mestiza Consciousness: Anzaldúa's *Borderlands/La Frontera*," Erika Aigner-Varoz argues that Anzaldúa reclaimed the mythological snake from its male-centered past (52). Anzaldúa's description of the alien as a "serpent" in her alien reclamation project is therefore significant, showing how her many metaphors would often overlap.

5   In *Borderlands/La Frontera: The New Mestiza*, "alien" at times refers to the social and political category of the alien, not to extraterrestrials (e.g., 39, 42, 70). Even in these cases, however, Anzaldúa typically makes use of the variety of meanings of the term "alien" to connect multiple aspects of reality and to express a vision of solidarity. In addition, this usage points to the political and sociological issues that are evoked when she does use the space alien.

6   Vasconcelos's idea of a future more highly evolved mixed race as well as the inclusion of the term "cosmic" in this formulation are tied to his interest in Theosophy, a nineteenth-century occultist religion founded by Helena Blavatsky. Tace Hedrick notes that at the time of writing *La raza cósmica*, "Vasconcelos, who was a member of a theosophist lodge in Mexico City, followed the current enthusiasm for uses of the term *cosmic*" (70). Vasconcelos's concept of *la raza cósmica* mirrors the cosmology of Theosophy that posited a "racial and planetary development over vast cosmic cycles" and pronounced that there were many ages or "races" of humanity, and that a more evolved race of humanity will come in the future (Goodrick-Clarke 302). What Vasconcelos brought to Theosophy was his emphasis on Latin America as the center of the future racial and cosmic development.

7   *Jotería* derives from the term *Joto*, meaning queer, and like queer it has become something of a positive reappropriation.

Chapter 3 Reclaiming the Space Alien

1 For a summation of the law, see https://www.findlaw.com/immigration /immigration-laws-and-resources/arizona-immigration-law-s-b-1070.html.

2 The text of the law can be found here: https://en.wikisource.org/wiki/California _Proposition_187_(1994).

3 The repeal can be found here: http://leginfo.legislature.ca.gov/faces /billNavClient.xhtml?bill_id=201320140SB396.

4 This concept about the tabloids proclaiming the actual truth even though it is absurd is present in the film *Men in Black* when Agent K checks the tabloid *Weekly World News* (famous for its reporting on the "Bat Boy") to get the information he needs. He says to Agent J: "Best damn investigative reporting on the planet. But hey, go ahead, read the *New York Times* if you want. They get lucky sometimes."

Chapter 4 Aliens in a Strange Land

1 Double allegorical readings of space alien narratives are common given the ability of the alien figure to represent all sorts of human groups. The South African film *District 9* (2009), for example, overtly correlates the space alien with immigrants, and yet it also expresses another correlation between the space aliens and the victims of apartheid. How the two readings relate to one another gives the film a complexity as well as having political ramifications since the duality can produce sympathy for immigrants through their correlation with the victims of apartheid or it can ignore the politically charged situation of recent immigrants for the more acceptable allegory of apartheid.

Chapter 5 The Unbearable Enlightenment of the Space Alien

1 One of the earliest works of Latinx science fiction featuring an enlightened space alien is Arthur Tenorio's *Blessing from Above* (1971), which tells the story of an alien who comes to Earth and secretly aids a fictional African nation in becoming prosperous.

2 The original published version used here has only two parts. The current e-book version available online has three "books." The e-book version also has edited out the eccentric use of ellipses in the original version, a choice that I very much oppose as it takes away the sense of a stream of consciousness that is integral to the story.

3 As Roth also shows, a number of the early contactees were overt White suprema- cists, and along with the Aryan enlightened space aliens, there were "intruders" who were thinly veiled allegories of Jews and their "invasion" of Western culture (56–57).

4 The satirical performance troupe Culture Clash was founded on May 5, 1984, in San Francisco's Mission District. The primary members of the group are Richard Montoya, Ric Salinas, and Herbert Siguenza.

Chapter 6 Space Aliens and the Discovery of Horror

1 The reference to Hemingway's "A Clean, Well-Lighted Place" (1933) indicates a certain ability of Torres to fend off the truth of life with unthinking habit, as does the protagonist in "A Clean, Well-Lighted Place."

2 For further discussion of how the characters are organized to create dramatic irony, see my essay "Sex with Aliens: Dramatic Irony in Daína Chaviano's 'The Annunciation,'" in *The Routledge Companion to Gender, Sex and Latin American Culture* (2018).

Chapter 7 *La conciencia Chupacabras*

1 Other later works include the popular novel *The Sparrow* (1996) by Mary Doria Russell, the film version of *Contact* (1997), and more recently, the short story "The Great Silence" (2016) by Ted Chiang. For a discussion of a recent Puerto Rican science fiction film not set at Arecibo, see my essay *"Extra Terrestres* and the Politics of Scientific Realism," in *Latinx Ciné: Filmmaking, Production, and Consumption in the 21st Century* (2019).

2 Originally under control of Cornell University, Arecibo Observatory is now jointly run by the University of Central Florida, Yang Enterprises, and Ana G. Mendez University. It is owned, however, by the U.S.-based National Science Foundation. On November 19, 2020, the foundation made the announcement that the observatory had suffered irreparable damage and would be decommissioned ("NSF Begins Planning for Decommissioning of Arecibo Observatory's 305-Meter Telescope Due to Safety Concerns").

3 For a more detailed account of the beginnings of the Chupacabras phenomenon in Puerto Rico, the following are helpful: *Tracking the Chupacabra: The Vampire Beast in Fact, Fiction, and Folklore* (Radford 2011), "Imperial Secrets: Vampires and Nationhood in Puerto Rico" (Derby 2008), and *Governing Spirits: Religion, Miracles, and Spectacles in Cuba and Puerto Rico, 1898–1956* (Román 2007).

4 The Chupacabras has been well represented in youth literature. See, for example, Xavier Garza's *Vincent Ventura and the Mystery of the Chupacabras* (2018), *The Chupacabras of the Río Grande* (2019), by Adam Gidwitz, David Bowles, and Hatem Aly, and *The Adventures of Chupacabra Charlie* (Aldama 2020).

Works Cited

Adamski, George. *Inside the Flying Saucers*. Abelard-Shuman, 1955.

Adamski, George, and Demond Leslie. *Flying Saucers Have Landed*. British Book Centre, 1953.

Aigner-Varoz, Erika. "Metaphors of a Mestiza Consciousness: Anzaldúa's *Borderlands/La Frontera*." *MELUS*, vol. 25, no. 2, 2000, pp. 48–62.

Alcaraz, Lalo. *La Cucaracha*. Andrews McMeel, 2004.

———. *Migra Mouse: Political Cartoons on Immigration*. RDV/Akashic Books, 2004.

———. *Pocho Magazine*, no. 7. Wisconsin Library Systems, copy of original zine, 1994.

Alcaraz, Lalo, and Ilan Stavans. *Latino USA: A Cartoon History*. Basic Books, 2000.

Aldama, Frederick Luis. *The Adventures of Chupacabra Charlie*. Mad Creek Books, 2020.

———. Preface. *The Routledge Concise History of Latino/a Literature*, edited by Frederick Luis Aldama, Routledge, 2013, pp. ix–xvi.

Alemán, Jesse. "Days of the (Un)Dead: Vampires, Zombies, and Other Forms of Chicano/a Horror in Film." *Latinos and Narrative Media: Participation and Portrayal*, edited by Frederick Luis Aldama, Palgrave Macmillan, 2013, pp. 49–69.

Alien. Directed by Ridley Scott, 20th Century Fox, 1979.

Als, Hilton. "Ghosts in the House: How Toni Morrison Fostered a Generation of Black Writers." *New Yorker*, October 20, 2003, https://www.newyorker.com/magazine/2003/10/27/ghosts-in-the-house. Accessed December 1, 2019.

Anzaldúa, Gloria. "The Alien." Gloria Evangelina Anzaldúa Papers, Benson Latin American Collection, University of Texas Libraries, University of Texas at Austin, April 1980, Box 85, Folder 7.

———. *Borderlands/La Frontera: The New Mestiza*. Aunt Lute Books, 1987.

———. "Don't Give In, *Chicanita*." *Borderlands/La Frontera*, pp. 224–225.

———. "Interface." *Borderlands/La Frontera*, pp. 170–174.

———. "Lesbian Wit." An Interview with Jeffner Allen (late 1980s). *Interviews/Entrevistas: Gloria Anzaldúa*, Routledge, 2000, pp. 129–150.

———. "Making Choices: Writing, Spirituality, Sexuality, and the Political." An Interview with AnaLouise Keating (1991). *Interviews/Entrevistas*, pp. 152–176.

———. "La Prieta." *This Bridge Called My Back: Writings by Radical Women of Color*, edited by Cherríe L. Moraga and Gloria E. Anzaldúa, Third Woman Press, 1981, pp. 220–233.

———. "Spirituality, Sexuality, and the Body." An Interview with Linda Smuckler (1998). *The Gloria Anzaldúa Reader*, edited by AnaLouise Keating, Duke University Press, 2009, pp. 74–94.

"The Arecibo Message." Staff at the National Astronomy and Ionosphere Center. *Icarus*, no. 26, 1975, pp. 462–466.

Arellano, Gustavo. *Taco USA: How Mexican Food Conquered America*. Scribner, 2012.

Arnold, Kathleen R., editor. *Anti-Immigration in the United States: A Historical Encyclopedia*. Greenwood, 2011.

Avatar. Directed by James Cameron, 20th Century Fox, 2009.

Bader, Chris D. "The UFO Contact Movement from the 1950s to the Present." *Studies in Popular Culture*, vol. 17, no. 2, 1995, pp. 73–90.

Battaglia, Debbora. *E.T. Culture: Anthropology in Outerspaces*. Duke University Press, 2006.

Battlestar Galactica. Starring Edward James Olmos, NBCUniversal Television Group, 2004–2009.

Beirich, Heidi, and Mark Potok. "'Paleoconservatives' Decry Immigration." *Intelligence Report*, December 31, 2003, https://www.splcenter.org/fighting-hate/intelligence -report/2003/paleoconservatives-decry-immigration. Accessed May 13, 2019.

"The Birth of Jesus Foretold." Luke (1:26–38). *The Holy Bible*, New International Version, Biblica, 2011.

Bladerunner. Directed by Ridley Scott, written by Hampton Fancher and David Peoples, Warner Brothers, 1982.

Bowles, David. "Aztlán Liberated." *Chupacabra Vengeance*, Broken River Books, 2017, pp. 3–8.

———. "Chupacabra Genesis." *Medium*, April 20, 2017, https://medium.com/@ davidbowles/chupacabra-genesis-a503b1084596. Accessed May 26, 2020.

———. "Chupacabra Vengeance." *Chupacabra Vengeance*, Broken River Books, 2017, pp. 11–29.

Brescia, Pablo. "Code 51." Goodwin, *Latinx Rising*, pp. 11–15.

Burciaga, José Antonio. "The Great Taco War." *Drink Cultura: Chicanismo*, Capra Press, 1993, pp. 21–25

Burroughs, Edgar Rice. *A Princess of Mars*. 1917. Library of America, 2012.

Calvin, Ritch. "Isabella Ríos and *Victuum*: Speculating a Chicana Identity." *Americana*, vol. 3, no. 1, 2005, pp. 33–58.

Calvo-Quirós, William. "The Emancipatory Power of the Imaginary: Defining Chican@ Speculative Productions." Merla-Watson and Olguín, *Altermundos*, pp. 39–54.

Čapek, Karel. *R.U.R. (Rossum's Universal Robots)*. Translated by Claudia Novack, 1921, Penguin, 2004.

Cárdenas, Reyes. *Los Pachucos and La Flying Saucer*. 1974. *Reyes Cárdenas: Chicano Poet 1970–2010*, Aztlan Libre Press, 2013.

Carrington, André M. *Speculative Blackness: The Future of Race in Science Fiction*. University of Minnesota Press, 2016.

Cavendish, Margaret. *The Description of a New World, Called the Blazing-World*. 1666. Edited by Sara H. Mendelson, Broadview Press, 2016.

Chavez, Leo R. *The Latino Threat: Constructing Immigrants, Citizens, and the Nation*. Stanford University Press, 2008.

Chaviano, Daína. "The Annunciation." *Cosmos Latinos: An Anthology of Science Fiction from Latin America and Spain*, edited by Andrea L. Bell and Yolanda Molina-Gavilán, Wesleyan University Press, 2003, pp. 202–207.

Chavoya, C. Odine, and Rita Gonzalez, editors. *ASCO: A Retrospective, 1972–1987*. Los Angeles County Museum of Art, 2011.

Chupacabra vs. the Alamo. Directed by Terry Igram, performance by Erik Estrada, Echo Bridge Entertainment, 2013.

Córdova, Zoraida. "You Owe Me a Ride." *Star Wars: From a Certain Point of View*, Del Rey, 2017, pp. 157–168.

Corrales, Scott. *Chupacabras and Other Mysteries*. Greenleaf, 1997.

Culture Clash. *Bordertown: San Diego and Tijuana. Culture Clash in Americca*, first performed in 1998, Theatre Communications Group, 2003, pp. 1–64.

"Daína Chaviano." *Encyclopedia of Science Fiction*, www.sfencyclopedia.com/entry /chaviano_daina. Accessed May 14, 2019.

Dean, Jodi. *Aliens in America: Conspiracy Cultures from Outerspace to Cyberspace*. Cornell University Press, 1998.

Delany, Samuel R. "Racism and Science Fiction." *Dark Matter: A Century of Speculative Fiction from the African Diaspora*, edited by Sheree R. Thomas, Grand Central, 2000, pp. 383–397.

Delgadillo, Theresa. *Spiritual Mestizaje: Religion, Gender, Race, and Nation in Contemporary Chicana Narrative*. Duke University Press, 2011.

Denis, Nelson A. *War against All Puerto Ricans: Revolution and Terror in America's Colony*. Nation Books, 2015.

Derby, Lauren. "Imperial Secrets: Vampires and Nationhood in Puerto Rico." *Past and Present*, vol. 199, supplement 3, 2008, pp. 290–312.

Díaz, Junot. "Apocalypse: What Disasters Reveal." *Boston Review*, May 1, 2011, http:// bostonreview.net/junot-Díaz -apocalypse-haiti-earthquake. Accessed May 14, 2019.

———. *The Brief Wondrous Life of Oscar Wao*. Riverhead Books, 2007.

———. "Dream of the Red King." Introduction. *A Princess of Mars*, by Edgar Rice Burroughs. 1917. Library of America, 2012.

———. "Growing the Hell Up: From Middle Earth to NJ." *Guernica*, November 1, 2012, https://www.guernicamag.com/growing-the-hell-up-from-middle-earth-to -nj/. Accessed May 14, 2019.

———. "Junot Díaz Aims to Fulfill His Dream of Publishing Sci-Fi Novel with Monstro." *Geek's Guide to the Galaxy Culture*, October 3, 2012, https://www.wired .com/2012/10/geeks-guide-junot-Díaz/. Accessed May 14, 2019.

———. "Monstro." Goodwin, *Latinx Rising*, pp. 80–102.

District 9. Directed by Neill Blomkamp, Sony Pictures, 2009.

Downes v. Bidwell, 182 U.S. 244 (1901). *Justia: US Supreme Court*, https://supreme .justia.com/cases/federal/us/182/244/. Accessed November 23, 2019.

E.T. the Extra-Terrestrial. Directed by Steven Spielberg, Universal Pictures, 1982.

Fitting, Peter. "Estranged Invaders: *The War of the Worlds*." *Learning from Other Worlds: Estrangement, Cognition and the Politics of Science Fiction and Utopia*, edited by Patrick Parrinder, Liverpool University Press, 2000, pp. 127–145.

Flusser, Vilém. "Exile and Creativity." *The Freedom of the Migrant: Objections to Nationalism*, edited by Anke Finger, translated by Kenneth Kronenberg, University of Illinois Press, 2003, pp. 81–87.

Fontenelle, Bernard le Bovier de. *Conversations on the Plurality of Worlds*. Translated by H. A. Hargreaves, University of California Press, 1990.

Fuller, John. *The Interrupted Journey: Two Lost Hours "Aboard a Flying Saucer."* Dial Press, 1966.

García Ordaz, Daniel. "A Writer's Legacy," http://www.angelfire.com/poetry /mariachi/writing/Gloria.html. Accessed May 14, 2019.

González, Christopher. "Latino Sci-Fi: Cognition and Narrative Design in Alex Rivera's *Sleep Dealer.*" *Latinos and Narrative Media: Participation and Portrayal*, edited by Frederick Luis Aldama, Palgrave Macmillan, 2013, pp. 211–223.

Goodrick-Clarke, Nicholas. "Western Esoteric Traditions and Theosophy." *Handbook of the Theosophical Current*, edited by Olav Hammer and Mikael Rothstein, Brill, 2013, pp. 261–307.

Goodwin, Matthew David. "The Fusion of Migration and Science Fiction in Mexico, Puerto Rico, and the United States." University of Massachusetts, PhD dissertation, 2013.

——, editor. *Latinx Rising: An Anthology of Latinx Science Fiction and Fantasy.* 2017. Mad Creek Books, 2020.

——. "Sex with Aliens: Dramatic Irony in Daína Chaviano's 'The Annunciation.'" *The Routledge Companion to Gender, Sex and Latin American Culture*, edited by Frederick Luis Aldama, Routledge, 2018, pp. 129–138.

Gunn, James. 1972. *The Listeners.* Reputation Books, 2017.

Harvey, Robert C. "Introducing La Cucaracha." *La Cucaracha*, Andrews McMeel, 2004, pp. 5–6.

Hawking, Stephen. "Stephen Hawking Warns over Making Contact with Aliens." *BBC News*, April 25, 2010, http://news.bbc.co.uk/2/hi/uk_news/8642558.stm. Accessed May 8, 2020.

Hedrick, Tace. "Queering the Cosmic Race: Esotericism, Mestizaje, and Sexuality in the Work of Gabriela Mistral and Gloria Anzaldúa." *Aztlán: A Journal of Chicano Studies*, vol. 34, no. 2, 2009, pp. 67–98.

Helguera, Jesus de la. "Amor Indio." *Velvet Barrios: Popular Culture and Chicana/o Sexualities*, edited by Alicia Gaspar de Alba, Palgrave Macmillan, 2003, p. 300.

Hemingway, Ernest. 1933. "A Clean, Well-Lighted Place." *The Complete Short Stories of Ernest Hemingway*, Finca Vigía Edition, Scribner, 2003, pp. 288–291.

Hernandez, Carlos. "American Moat." *The Assimilated Cuban's Guide to Quantum Santeria.* Rosarium, 2016, pp. 200–210.

Hernández, Robb. *Mundos Alternos: Art and Science Fiction in the Americas*, edited by Robb Hernández and Tyler Stallings, UCR ARTSbloc, 2017.

Hicks, Heather J. "Suits vs. Skins: Immigration and Race in Men in Black." *Arizona Quarterly*, vol. 63, no. 2, 2007, pp. 109–136.

Hogan, Ernest. "Chicanonautica: Cortez on Jupiter, Hogan vs. Nueva York." *La Bloga*, March 1, 2012, https://labloga.blogspot.com/2012/03/chicanonautica-cortez -on-jupiter-hogan.html. Accessed May 13, 2019.

——. *Cortez on Jupiter.* Tor, 1990.

——. *High Aztech.* Tor, 1992.

——. *Smoking Mirror Blues.* Wordcraft of Oregon, 2001.

"Hotel Dick." *3rd Rock from the Sun*, written by Bob Kushell, directed by Terry Hughes, season 2, episode 3, Carsey-Werner, September 29, 1996.

Huang, Betsy. *Contesting Genres in Contemporary Asian American Fiction.* Palgrave Macmillan, 2010.

Huhndorf, Shari M. *Going Native: Indians in the American Cultural Imagination.* Cornell University Press, 2001.

Independence Day. Directed by Ronald Emmerich, 20th Century Fox, 1996.

Irving, Washington. *A History of New-York from the Beginning of the World to the End of the Dutch Dynasty*. 1809. 4th American ed., C.S. Van Winkle, 1824.

Iyengar, Sujata. "Royalist, Romancist, Racialist: Rank, Gender, and Race in the Science and Fiction of Margaret Cavendish." *ELH*, vol. 69, no. 3, Fall 2002, pp. 649–672.

James, Edward. "Sheri S. Tepper." *Aliens in Popular Culture*, edited by Michael M. Levy and Farah Mendlesohn, Greenwood, 2019, pp. 262–264.

Kuhn, Annette. "Border Crossing." *Sight and Sound*, vol. 2, no. 3, 1992, p. 13.

Kydd, Elspeth. "Differences: *The X-Files*, Race and the White Norm." *Journal of Film and Video*, vol. 53, no. 4, Winter 2001–2002, pp. 72–82.

"Latino Science Fiction." Matthew Goodwin and Ilan Stavans, *Oxford Bibliographies Online*, 2016, https://www.oxfordbibliographies.com/view/document/obo -9780199913701/obo-9780199913701-0112.xml. Accessed May 13, 2019.

Laviera, Tato. *AmeRícan*. Arte Público Press, 1985.

———. *La Carreta Made a U-turn*. Arte Público Press, 1979.

———. *Mixturao and Other Poems*. Arte Público Press, 2008.

———. "Puerto Rico's Chupacabras." *Mixturao and Other Poems*, Arte Publico Press, 2008, pp. 12–16.

Le Guin, Ursula. "American SF and the Other." *Science Fiction Studies*, vol. 2, no. 7, 1975, https://www.depauw.edu/sfs/backissues/7/leguin7art.htm. Accessed May 13, 2019.

Lem, Stanislaw. *Solaris*. Translated by Bill Johnston, Pro Auctore Wojciech Zemek, 2014.

Lepselter, Susan. *Resonance of Unseen Things: Poetics, Power, Captivity, and UFOs in the American Uncanny*. University of Michigan Press, 2016.

"Little Green Men." *The X-Files*, created by Chris Carter, season 2, episode 1, Ten Thirteen Productions, September 16, 1994.

Loza, Susana. "Playing Alien in Post-Racial Times." *Monster Culture in the 21st Century: A Reader*, edited by Marina Levina and Diem-My T. Bui, Bloomsbury Academic, 2013, pp. 53–72.

Lucian of Samosata. *A True History. Lucian: Selected Dialogues*. Translated by C. D. N. Costa, Oxford University Press, 2005, pp. 203–233.

Luis, William. "From New York to the World: An Interview with Tato Laviera." *Callaloo*, vol. 15, no. 4, 1992, pp. 1022–1033.

Maguire, Emily A. "Science Fiction." *The Routledge Companion to Latino/a Literature*, edited by Suzanne Bostand and Frances R. Aparicio, Routledge, 2013, pp. 351–360.

Marcum, Carl. "SciFi-ku." Goodwin, *Latinx Rising*, p. 237.

Marentes, Luis A. *José Vasconcelos and the Writing of the Mexican Revolution*. Twayne, 2000.

Marez, Curtis. "Aliens and Indians: Science Fiction, Prophetic Photography and Near-Future Visions." *Journal of Visual Culture*, vol. 3, no. 3, 2004, pp. 336–352.

———. *Farm Worker Futurism: Speculative Technologies of Resistance*. University of Minnesota Press, 2016.

Marqués, René. *La carreta: drama en rres actos*. Rio Piedras, Editorial Cultural, 1983. First performed in 1954.

Massey, Douglas, et al. *Beyond Smoke and Mirrors: Mexican Immigration in an Era of Economic Integration*. Russell Sage Foundation, 2002.

Men in Black. Directed by Barry Sonnenfeld, Sony Pictures, 1997.

Merla-Watson, Cathryn J. "Haunted by Voices: Historical Im/Materialism and Gloria Anzaldúa's Mestiza Consciousness." *El Mundo Zurdo 3 Selected Works from the 2012 Meeting of the Society for the Study of Gloria Anzaldúa*, edited by Larissa M. Mercado-López et al., Aunt Lute Books, e-book, 2013.

———. "Latinofuturism." *Oxford Research Encyclopedias*, 2019, https://oxfordre.com /literature/oso/viewentry/10.1093$002facrefore$002f9780190201098.001 .0001$002facrefore-9780190201098-e-648#acrefore-9780190201098-e-648-div1-3. Accessed May 16, 2019.

Merla-Watson, Cathryn Josefina, and B. V. Olguín, editors. *Altermundos: Latin@ Speculative Literature, Film, and Popular Culture*. UCLA Chicano Studies Research Center Press, 2017.

Mexican Werewolf in Texas. Directed by Scott Maginnis, Turning Point Productions, 2005.

Molina, Laura. *Amor Alien*. 2004. *Mundos Alternos: Art and Science Fiction in the Americas*, edited by Robb Hernández and Tyler Stallings, UCR ARTSbloc, 2017, p. 113.

———. "Artist's Statement." *Naked Dave*, https://nakeddave.com/NakedDave03.html. Accessed May 30, 2020.

———. "Dave Stevens: Naked Dave." *Naked Dave*, https://web.archive.org/web /20010303061925/http://www.nakeddave.com/davePart2.html. Accessed September 4, 2019.

———. "The Green Lady." 2007. *Naked Dave*, https://nakeddave.com/NakedDave01 .html. Accessed May 30, 2019.

———. "Vampirella Cosplay." *Facebook*, June 19, 2019, https://www.facebook.com /laura.molina/posts/10156394466828106. Accessed May 30, 2020.

Molina-Gavilán, Yolanda. "Eugenic Orgasms? A Fresh Look at Christian Mithology: Daína Chaviano's 'The Annunciation.'" *Daína Chaviano, Author*, www .dainachaviano.com/paper.php?lang=en&item=45#.WW1DkumQxPYNarvaez. Accessed May 14, 2019.

Monk, Patricia. *Alien Theory: The Alien as Archetype in the Science Fiction Short Story*. Scarecrow Press, 2006.

Moraga, Cherrie. *The Hungry Woman: A Mexican Medea*. West End Press, 2001.

Morales, Alejandro. *The Rag Doll Plagues*. Arte Publico Press, 1991.

"El Mundo Gira." *The X-Files*, created by Chris Carter, season 4, episode 11, Ten Thirteen Productions, January 12, 1997.

Napier, Susan. *The Fantastic in Modern Japanese Literature: The Subversion of Modernity*. Routledge, 2005.

Narvaez, Richie. "Room for Rent." Goodwin, *Latinx Rising*, pp. 103–113.

"NSF Begins Planning for Decommissioning of Arecibo Observatory's 305-Meter Telescope Due to Safety Concerns." National Science Foundation, November 19, 2020. https://www.nsf.gov/news/news_summ.jsp?cntn_id=301674. Accessed December 9, 2020.

Older, Daniel José. *Last Shot (Star Wars): A Han and Lando Novel*, Del Rey, 2018.

Older, Malka. *Infomocracy: Book One of the Centenal Cycle*. Tor, 2016.

———. *Null States: Book Two of the Centenal Cycle*. Tor, 2017.

———. *State Tectonics: Book Three of the Centenal Cycle*. Tor, 2018.

Olmos, Edward James. "Battlestar Galactica—Latinos in Sci Fi." *YouTube*, uploaded by the Paley Center for Media, March 4, 2009, https://www.youtube.com/watch?v =1F9axZIBArM. Accessed November 20, 2019.

———. *Dangerous Days: Making Blade Runner. Blade Runner: Special Edition*, Warner Home Video, "First Blush: Assembling the Cast," 20:33–20:37, 2007, DVD.

Omi, Michael, and Howard Winant. *Racial Formation in the United States*. 3rd ed., Routledge, 2015.

Orchard, William. "Trans-American Popular Forms of Latina/o Literature." *The Cambridge History of Latina/o American Literature*, edited by John Morán González and Laura Lomas, Cambridge University Press, 2018, pp. 636–656.

Pérez, Juan Manuel. "Open Letter from the Chupacabra." *Sex, Lies, and Chupacabras*, House of the Fighting Chupacabras Press, e-book, 2015.

Peynado, Brenda. "The Kite Maker." Tor.com, August 29, 2018, https://www.tor .com/2018/08/29/the-kite-maker-brenda-peynado/. Accessed May 14, 2019.

Poblete, Juan. "The Archeology of the Post-Social in the Comics of Lalo Alcaraz: *La Cucaracha* and *Migra Mouse*: Political Cartoons on Immigration." *Graphic Borders: Latino Comic Books Past, Present, and Future*, edited by Frederick Luis Aldama and Christopher González, University of Texas Press, 2016, pp. 158–174.

Radford, Benjamin. *Tracking the Chupacabra: The Vampire Beast in Fact, Fiction, and Folklore*. University of New Mexico Press, 2011.

Ramírez, Catherine S. "Cyborg Feminism: The Science Fiction of Octavia E. Butler and Gloria Anzaldúa." *Reload: Rethinking Women + Cyberculture*, edited by Mary Flanagan and Austin Booth, MIT Press, 2002, pp. 374–402.

———. "Deus ex Machina: Tradition, Technology, and the Chicanafuturist Art of Marion C. Martinez." *Aztlán: A Journal of Chicano Studies*, vol. 29, no. 2, 2004, pp. 55–92.

Ramírez Berg, Charles. *Latino Images in Film: Stereotypes, Subversion, Resistance*. University of Texas Press, 2002.

Rennie, Mike. "Heaven's Gate." *Aliens in Popular Culture*, edited by Michael M. Levy and Farah Mendlesohn, Greenwood, 2019, pp. 144–147.

Rieder, John. *Colonialism and the Emergence of Science Fiction*. Wesleyan University Press, 2008.

Rios, Isabella (Diana López). *Victuum*. Diana-Etna, 1976.

———. *Victuum*. Diana-Etna, 1976. Kindle.

Rivera, Lysa. "Los Atravesados: Guillermo Gómez-Peña's Ethno-cyborgs." *Aztlan: A Journal of Chicano Studies*, vol. 31, no. 1, 2010, pp. 103–133.

———. "Future Histories and Cyborg Labor: Reading Borderlands Science Fiction after NAFTA." *Science Fiction Studies*, vol. 39, no. 3, 2012, pp. 415–436.

Rivera, Mercurio D. "Dance of the Kawkawroons." *Across the Event Horizon*, New Con Press, 2013.

Román, Reinaldo L. *Governing Spirits: Religion, Miracles, and Spectacles in Cuba and Puerto Rico, 1898–1956*. University of North Carolina Press, 2007.

Roth, Christopher. "Ufology as Anthropology: Race, Extraterrestrials, and the Occult." *E.T. Culture: Anthropology in Outerspaces*, edited by Debbora Battaglia, Duke University Press, 2005, pp. 38–93.

Saldívar, Ramón. *Chicano Narrative: The Dialectics of Difference*. University of Wisconsin Press, 1990.

Sánchez, Rosaura, and Beatrice Pita. *Lunar Braceros 2125–2148*. Calaca Press, 2009.

Sandoval, Chela. "Foreword: Unfinished Words: The Crossing of Gloria Anzaldúa." *EntreMundos/AmongWorlds: New Perspectives on Gloria E. Anzaldúa*, edited by AnaLouise Keating, Palgrave, 2005, pp. xiii–xvi.

Sardar, Ziauddin. Introduction. *Aliens R Us: The Other in Science Fiction Cinema*, edited by Ziauddin Sardar and Sean Cubitt, Pluto Press, 2002, pp. 1–17.

Schwartz, A. Brad. *Broadcast Hysteria: Orson Welles's War of the Worlds and the Art of Fake News*. Farrar, Straus and Giroux, 2015.

Senarens, Luis. *The Frank Reade Library*. 1882–1898. Issues available online at https://catalog.hathitrust.org/Record/100707990. Accessed May 13, 2019.

Silko, Leslie Marmon. "Language and Literature from a Pueblo Indian Perspective." *English Literature: Opening Up the Canon*, edited by Leslie A. Fiedler and Houston A. Baker, Johns Hopkins University Press, 1981, pp. 54–72.

Solo: A Star Wars Story. Directed by Ron Howard, Walt Disney Studios, 2018.

Species. Directed by Roger Donaldson, Metro-Goldwyn-Mayer, 1995.

Star Trek. Created by Gene Roddenberry, Paramount, 1966–1969.

Star Wars: Episode I—The Phantom Menace. Directed by George Lucas, Lucasfilm, 1999.

Stavans, Ilan. *José Vasconcelos: The Prophet of Race*. Rutgers University Press, 2011.

———, general editor. *The Norton Anthology of Latino Literature*. W.W. Norton, 2011.

Stevens, Dave. *The Rocketeer*. 1982–1995.

Suvin, Darko. *Metamorphoses of Science Fiction: On the Poetics and History of a Literary Genre*. Yale University Press, 1979.

Toledano Redondo, Juan Carlos. "The Many Names of God: Christianity in Hispanic Caribbean Science Fiction." *Chasqui*, vol. 36, no. 1, 2007, pp. 33–47.

Tolentino, Madelyne. Interview with Scott Corrales. *Chupacabras and Other Mysteries*. Greenleaf Publications, 1997, pp. 31–59.

Tenorio, Arthur. *Blessing from Above*. West Las Vegas Schools' Press, 1971.

Valdez, Luis. "Los Vendidos." *Luis Valdez: Early Works: Actos, Bernabé and Pensamiento Serpentino*, Arte Publico, 1994, pp. 40–52.

Vasconcelos, José. *The Cosmic Race/La raza cósmica*. 1925. Translated by Didier T. Jaén, Johns Hopkins University Press, 1997.

Vourvoulias, Sabrina. *Ink*. Rosarium, 2018.

Welles, Orson. "The War of the Worlds." 1940. *The War of the Worlds: Mars' Invasion of Earth, Inciting Panic and Inspiring Terror, from H.G. Wells to Orson Welles and Beyond*. Sourcebooks, 2005, pp. 33–61.

Wells, H. G. *The War of the Worlds*. 1898. *A Critical Edition of* The War of the Worlds: *H.G. Wells's Scientific Romance*, edited by Harry M. Geduld and David Y. Hughes, Indiana University Press, 1993.

Womack, Ytasha L. *Afrofuturism: The World of Black Sci-Fi and Fantasy Culture*. Lawrence Hill Books, 2013.

Wood, Robin. *Hollywood from Vietnam to Reagan—and Beyond*. Expanded and revised ed., Columbia University Press, 2003.

The X-Files. Created by Chris Carter, Ten Thirteen Productions, 1993–2018.

Ybarra-Frausto, Tomás. "Primeros Pasos: First Steps toward an Operative Construct of Latino Art." *Our America: The Latino Presence in American Art*, Smithsonian American Art Museum, 2014, pp. 13–31.

Zagitt, Pedro. "Uninformed." Goodwin, *Latinx Rising*, pp. 16–17.

Index

Page references in *italics* refer to illustrations.

About the Author

MATTHEW DAVID GOODWIN is a visiting scholar at the Institute for Advanced Studies in Princeton. His work is focused on the ways that science fiction, fantasy, and digital culture are being used by Latinx authors. He is the editor of two anthologies: *Latinx Rising: An Anthology of Latinx Science Fiction and Fantasy* (2020) and *Speculative Fiction for Dreamers: A Latinx Anthology* (forthcoming 2021).

Printed and bound by CPI Group (UK) Ltd, Croydon, CR0 4YY

09/06/2025

14685738-0002